An artist's conspiracy

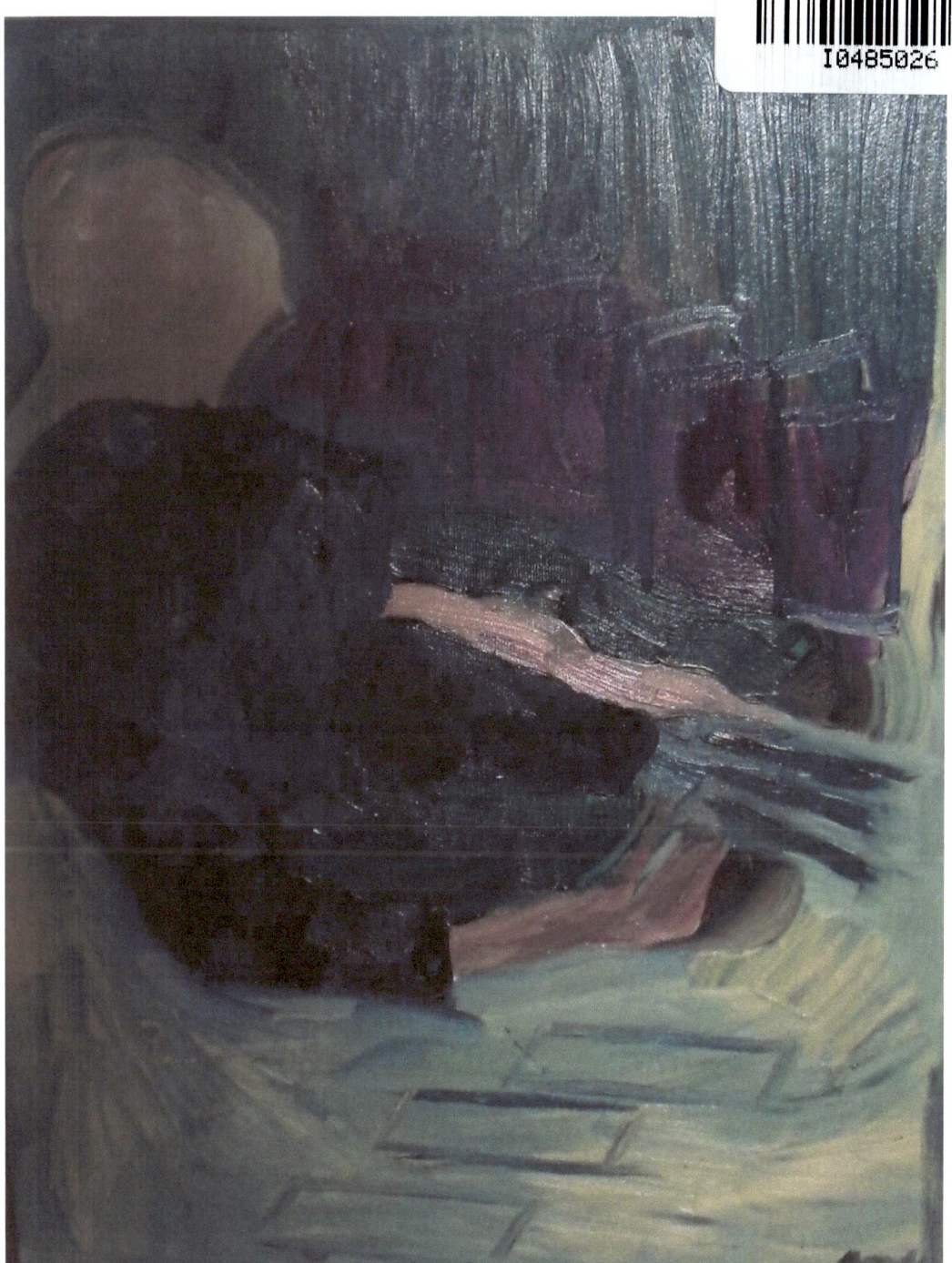

An artist has a hard life.Things don't often go his way, especially when he is trying to prevent an apocalypse.There are many things wrong with this world which most people seem to ignore.I'm not just talking about the bad news.The fundamental freedom of humanity is constantly threatened by an ever oppressive world.The world we inherited post 9/11 us full of fear and many conspiracies.There are so many inconsistancies in life it is almost as if we are being tricked into living a daily life which benefit's the 'system' and not ourselves.Basically we are becoming slaves and prisoners due to globalisation.Computer life is where most of the freedom occurs and where most of the new ideas are born..However this is now monitored due to terrorism.An artists job in the 21st century is to open doors

for people and draw their attention to the plight of humanity in the 21st century.What follows is my constant struggle as an entity to come up with ideas which are fresh and exciting as well as trying to suss out possible futures and ensure that the apocalyptic ones which I have seen are avoided.I will show you what I
mean.

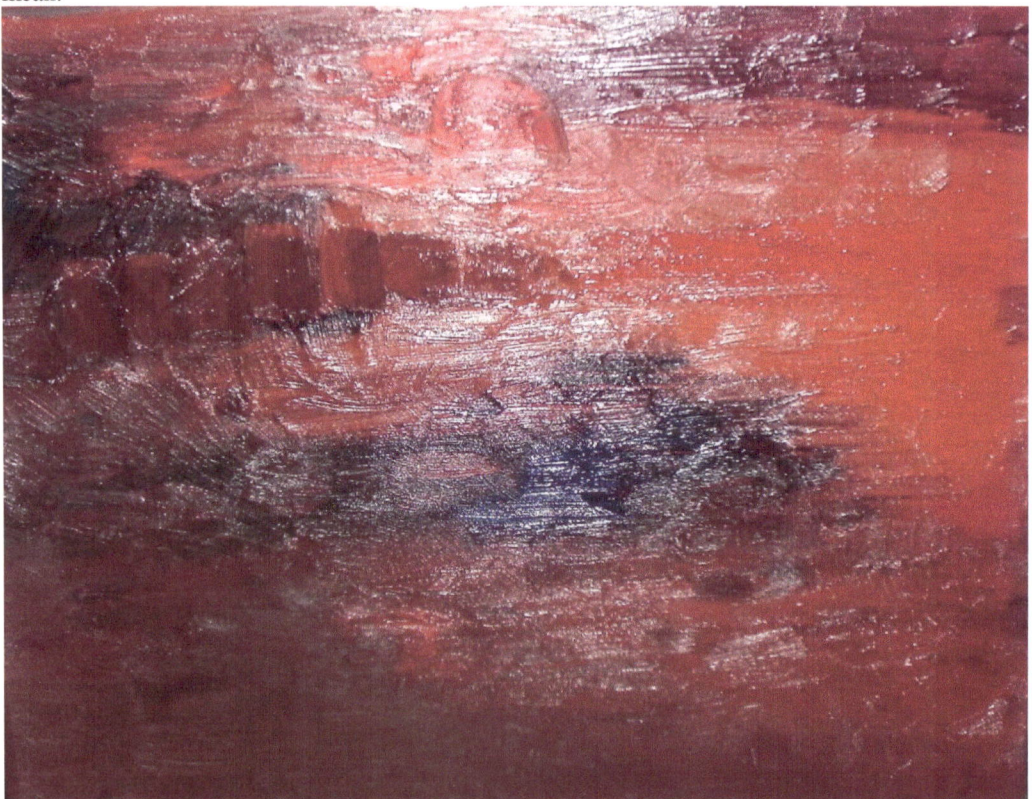

This is the worst case scenario called after the apocalypse.Everything destroyed, the world on fire.Total annilation of mankind.This passed a few months ago in 2010.It was a possibility.We live in the best of all possible worlds.There are possible and impossible particles.At the moment we have just enough possible particles to keep the world in motion however if the impossible particles are too many then another disaster like Haiti will occur or the financial crisis will occur.

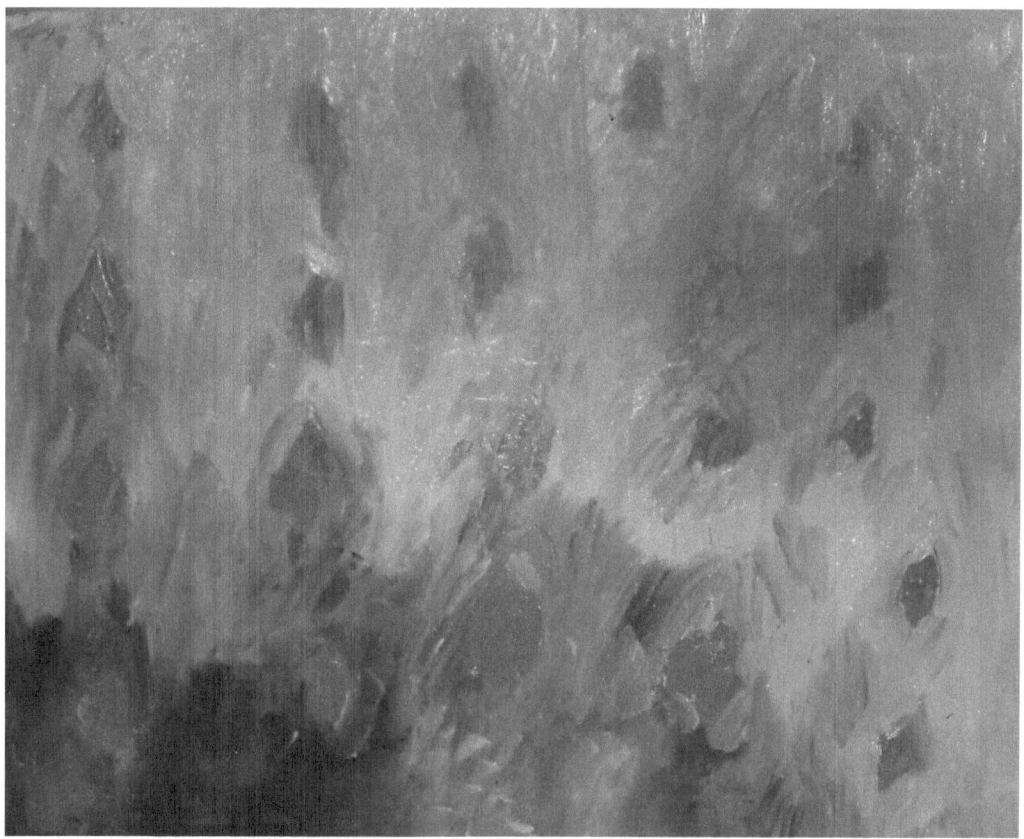

This is called ancestors.Our ancestors faced great tribulations like this but they survived and this is what gives me hope to work on.

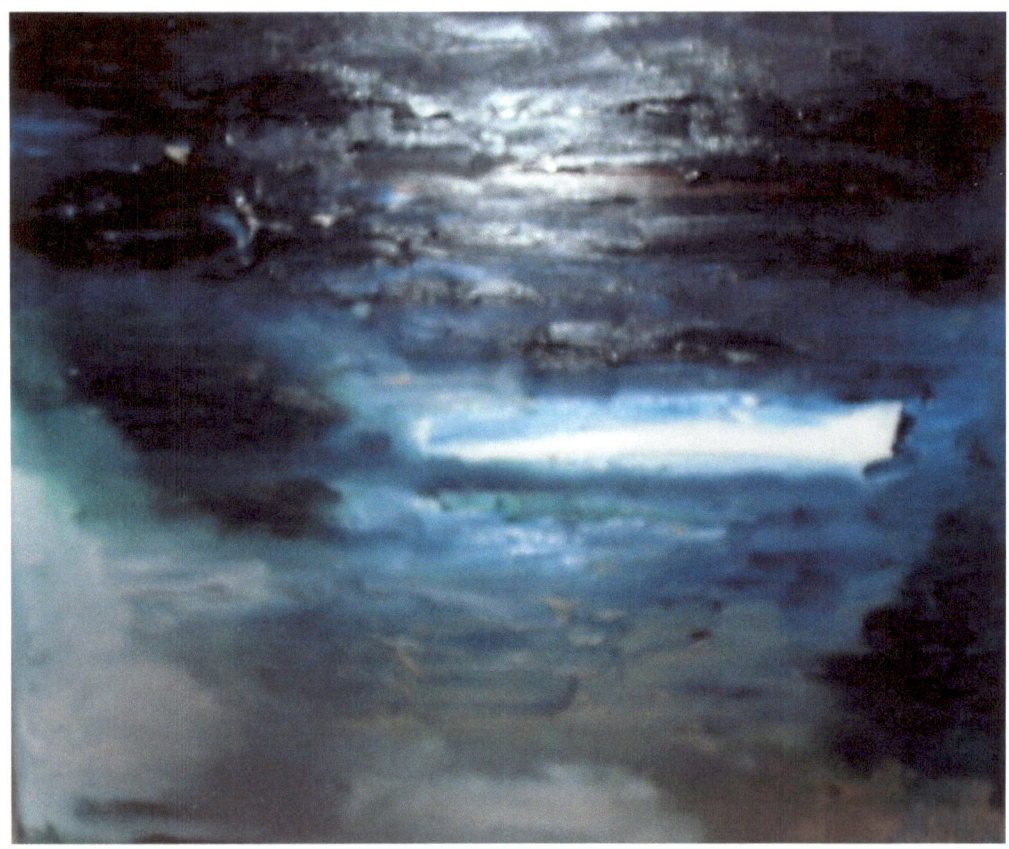

This is called endless skies and the world has changed so much so that it now seems bigger and more threatening to people.I rarely venture out not because of the people but because of the immensity of the endless skies above.It is becoming a hostile and intrusive almost as if the universe wants to take over the earths independence.The earth is moving through a troubled patch of universe which could be compared to a person crossing a galactic highway.This is a perilous time for the occupants of the earth as each possible future could be compared to an accident caused by a speeding car.So far so good for the earth to reach greener pastures we have to cross the second part of the road and hopefully in line with the Mayan prophecy of 2012 this is when we will reach the other side.It is called the black road.

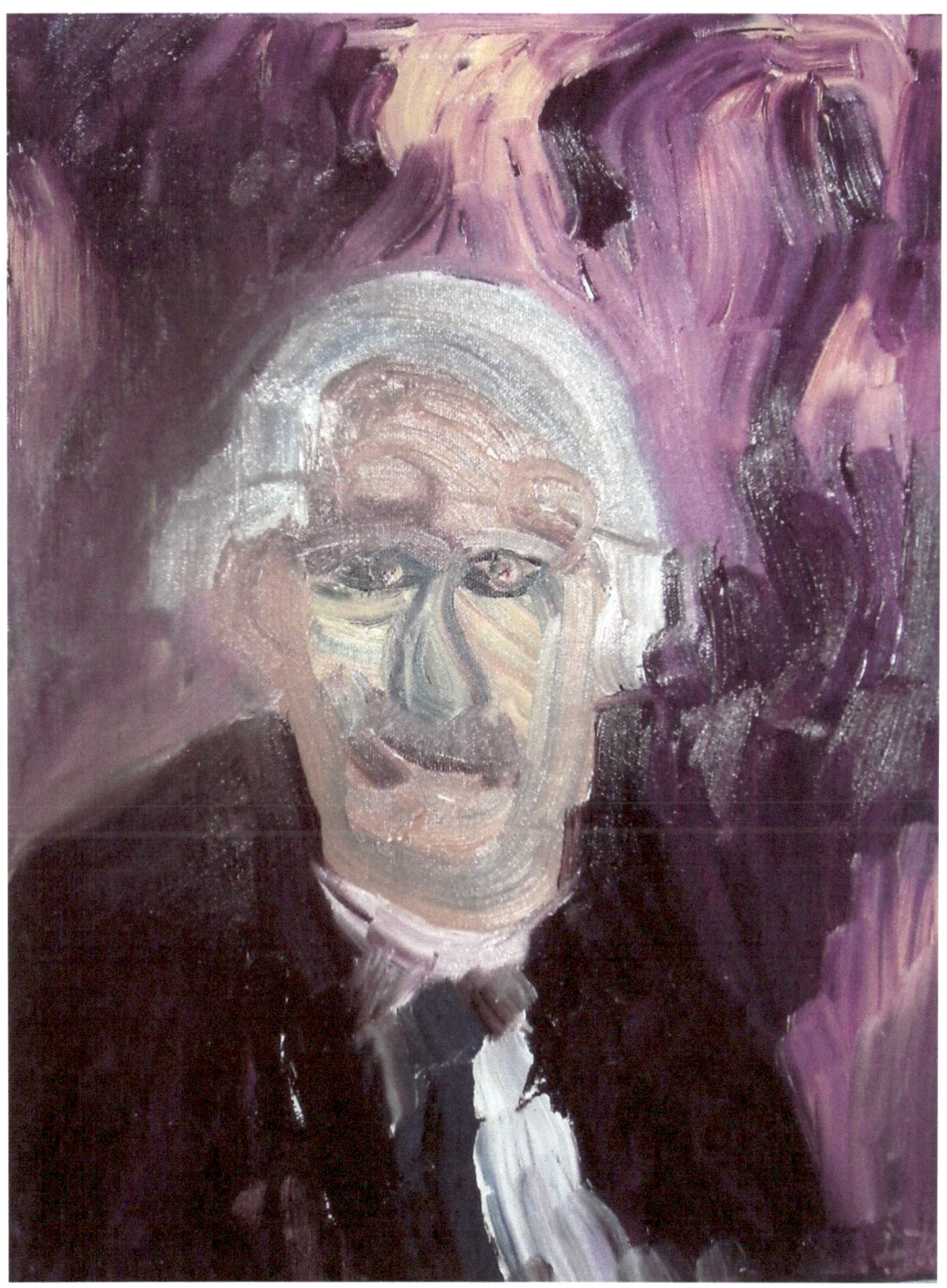

This is called Carl Yung.I have leaned on his knowledge so many times as I consider him to be the worlds best philosopher.

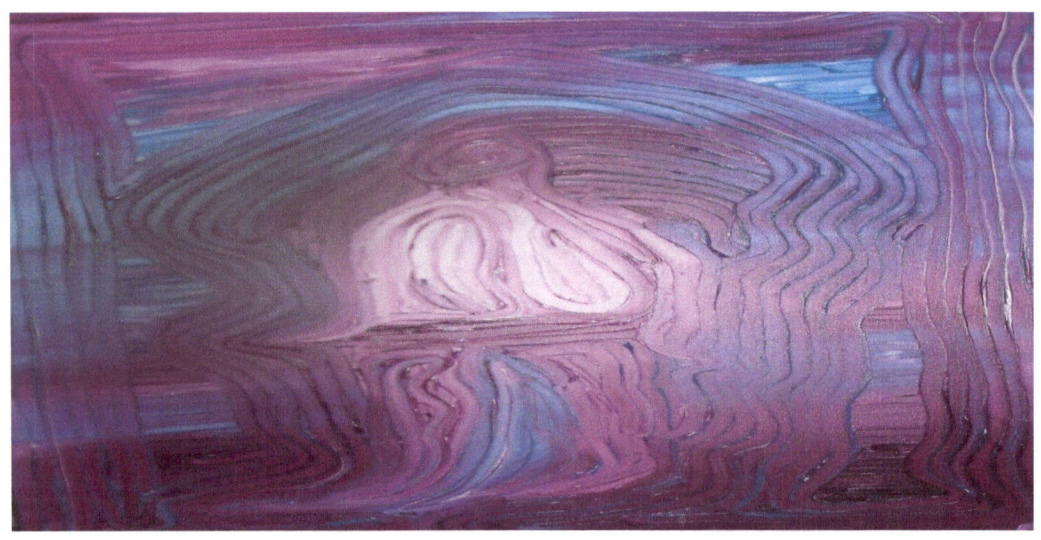

This is called Quezacoatal, the apocalypse man. It is an Aztec concept but still relevant as South American knowledge is becoming more important.

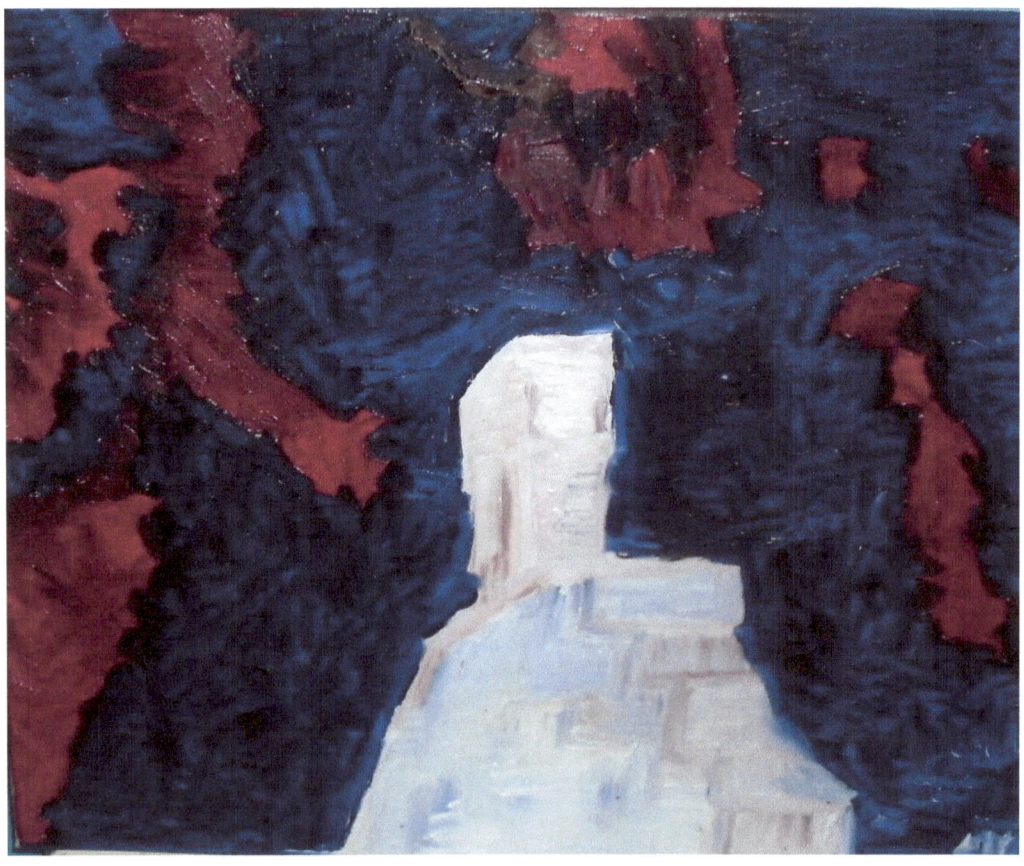

This is called Future chapel. It is part of the macro verse whose prescence in this world will endure until we have reached the other side.

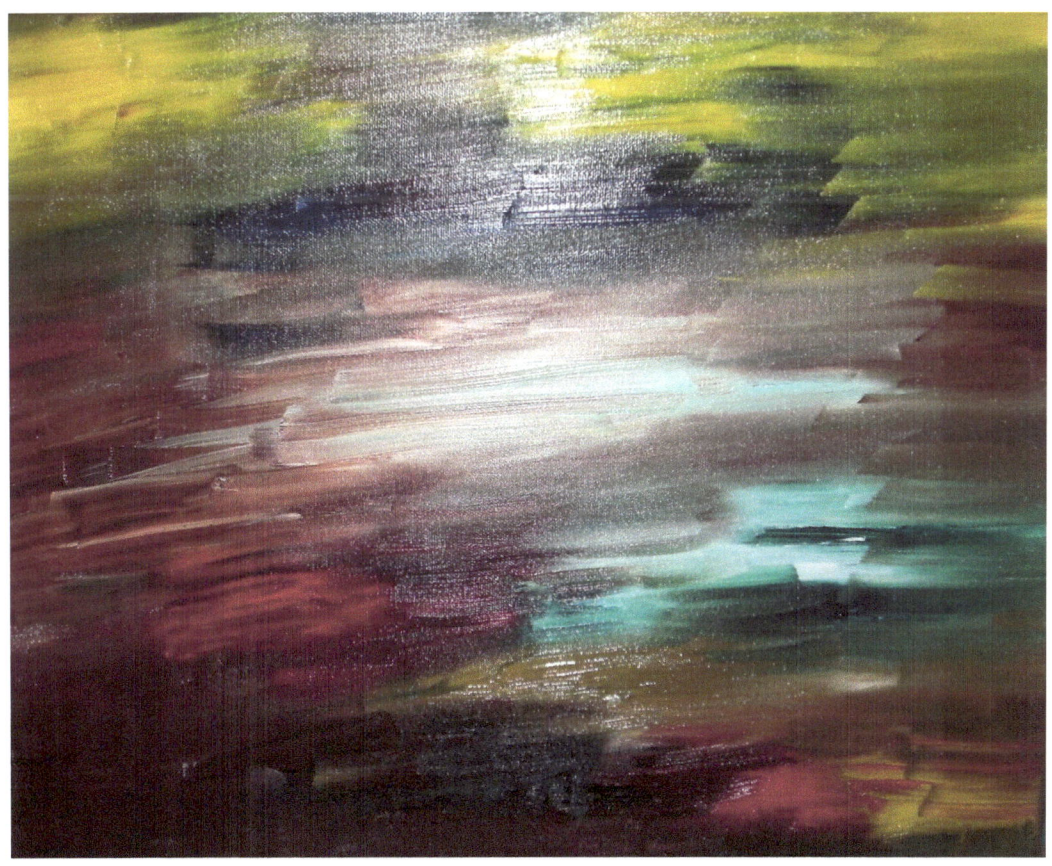

This is called in passing and to let life flow is important as clinging onto things causes resistance and leads to destruction.

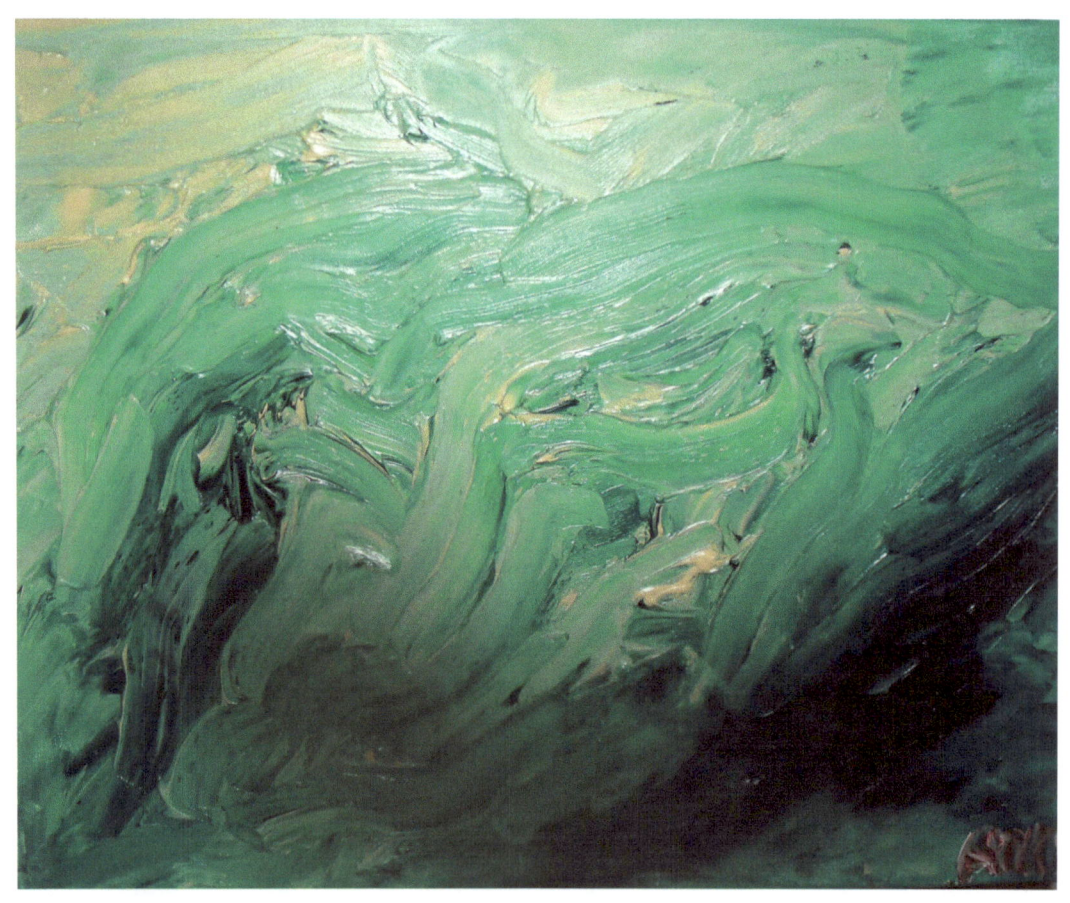

Finally though incongruous this is called sea monsters and was an attempt to rediscover Turners destiny as he seemed to carry the world through troubled times.This ends the chapter and is my attempt to show that whilst everyone is sleeping the governments of the world are constantly at work firstly finding possible futures and also trying to prevent any further damage to the systems they have created.

Chapter two.Glimmers of
hope.

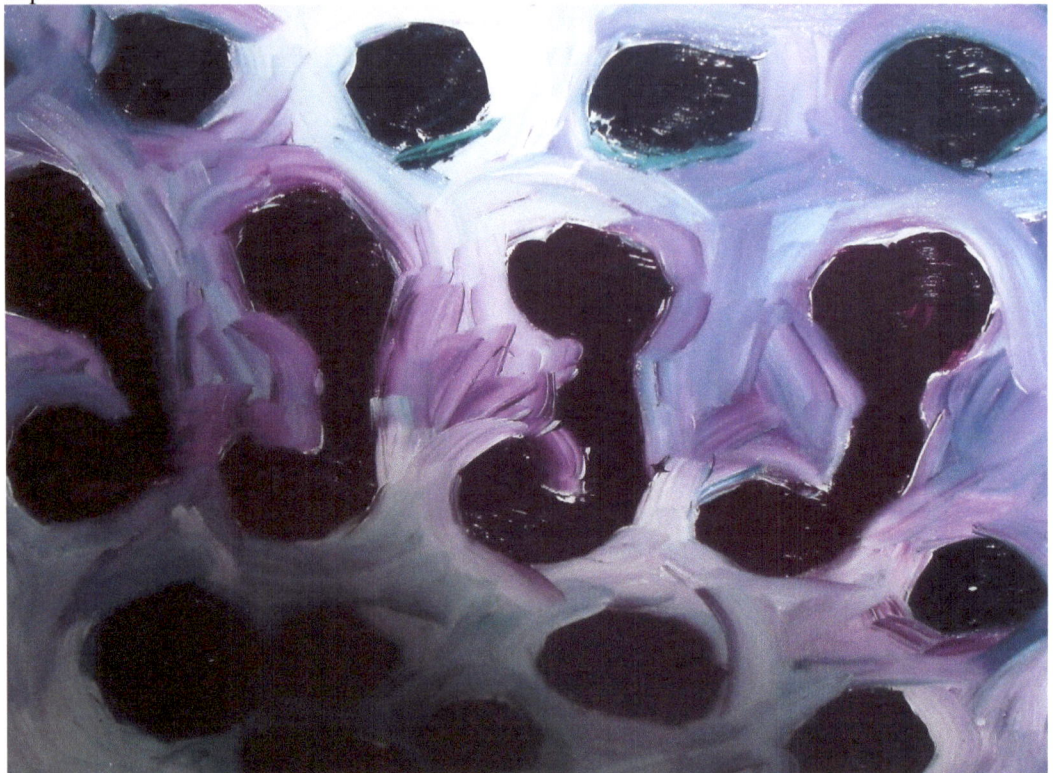

This is called Where Gods are born.This is the hope that after 2012 a new age of peace and security and freedom will come as renewable sources of energy are found and the intrusive controlling macro verse will relinquish its grip on earth.

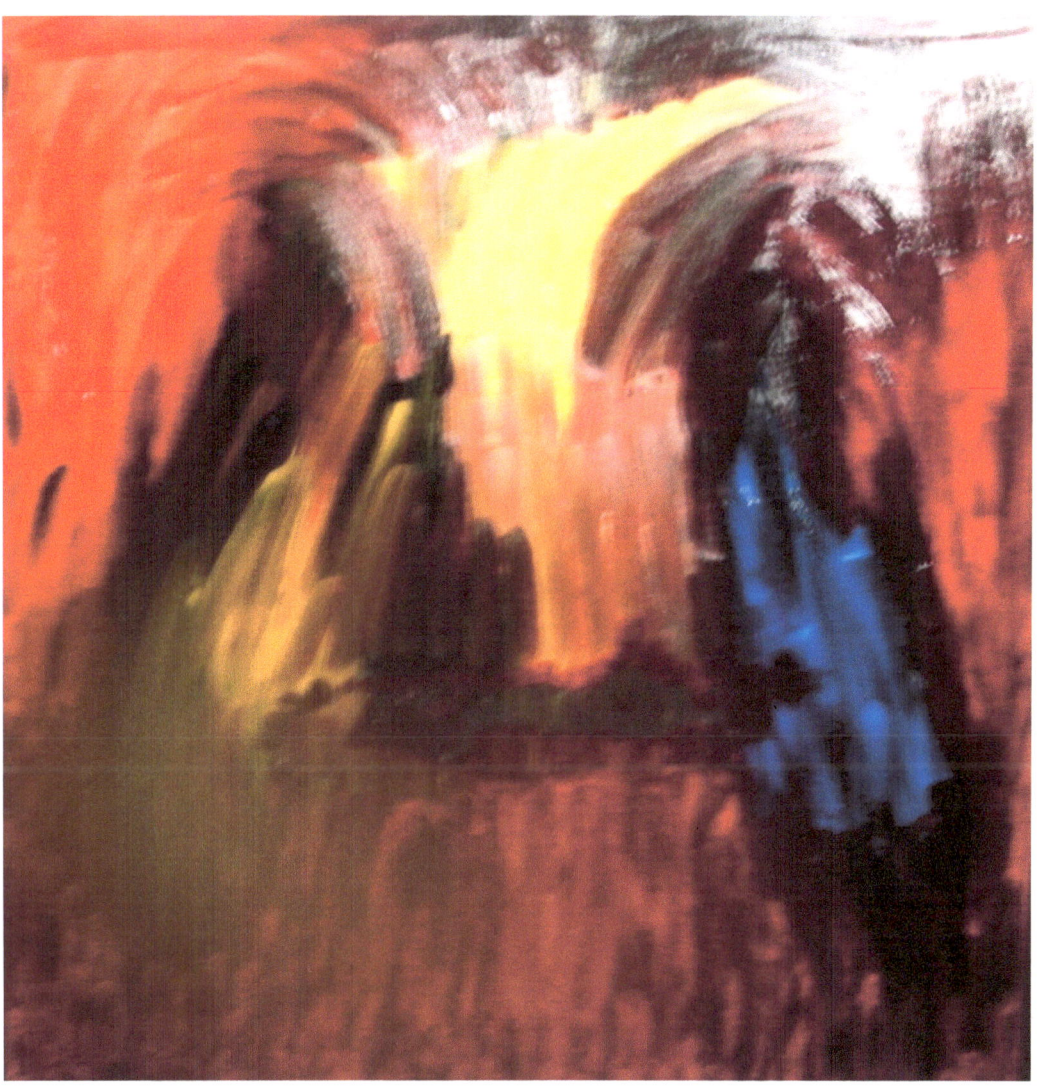

This is the wizard London.It is an entity in itself through which a channel was opened to the macro verse.It is a being so powerful that it controls the lives of millions of people.It has I believe an evil purpose and blackens the hearts of people under its influence.

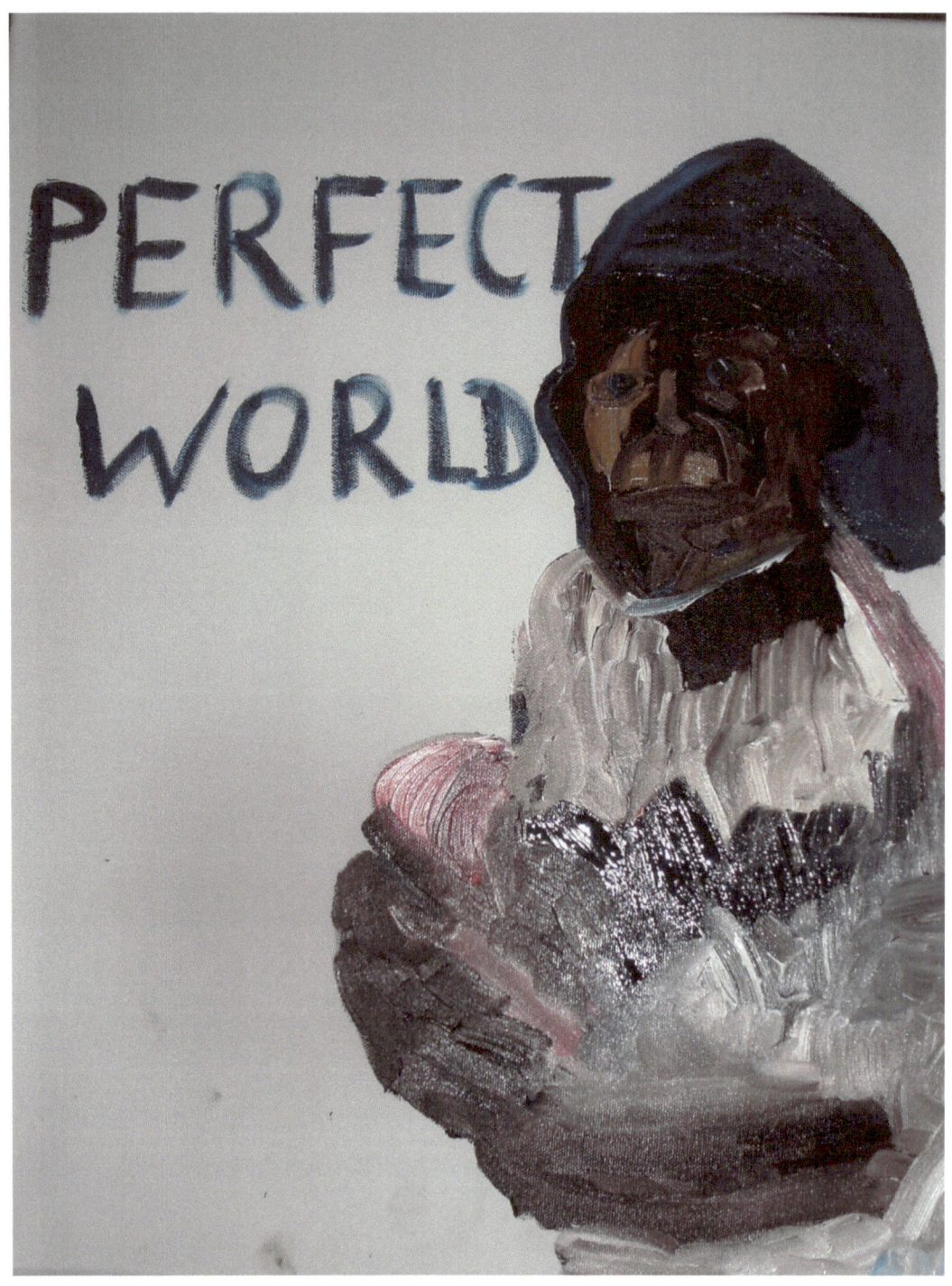

This is called Perfect World.Basically a tongue in cheek look at the policies of the World government which keeps so many people in need.

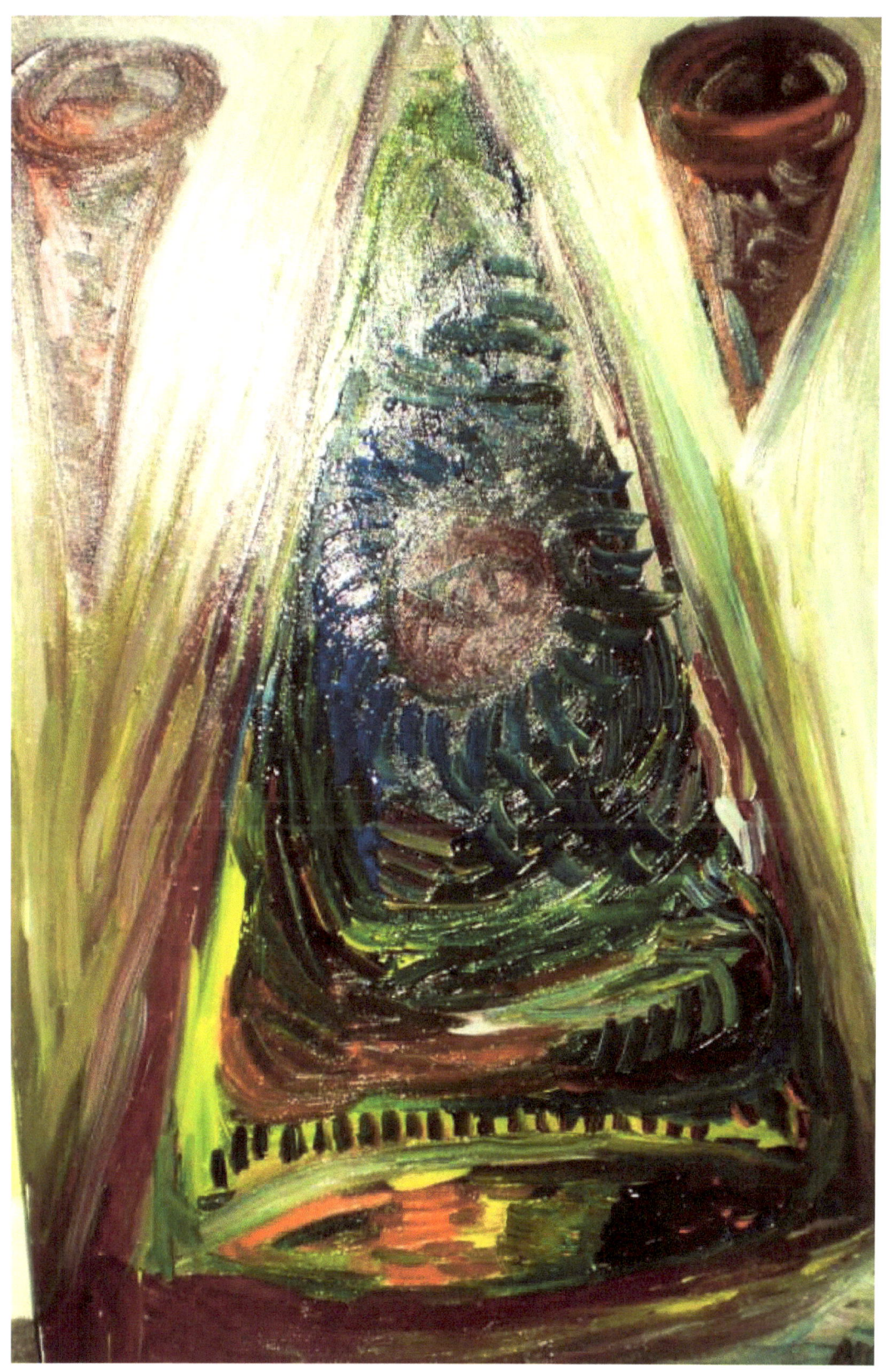

This is called money.Something which hypnotises so many people and it becomes like a God to them.

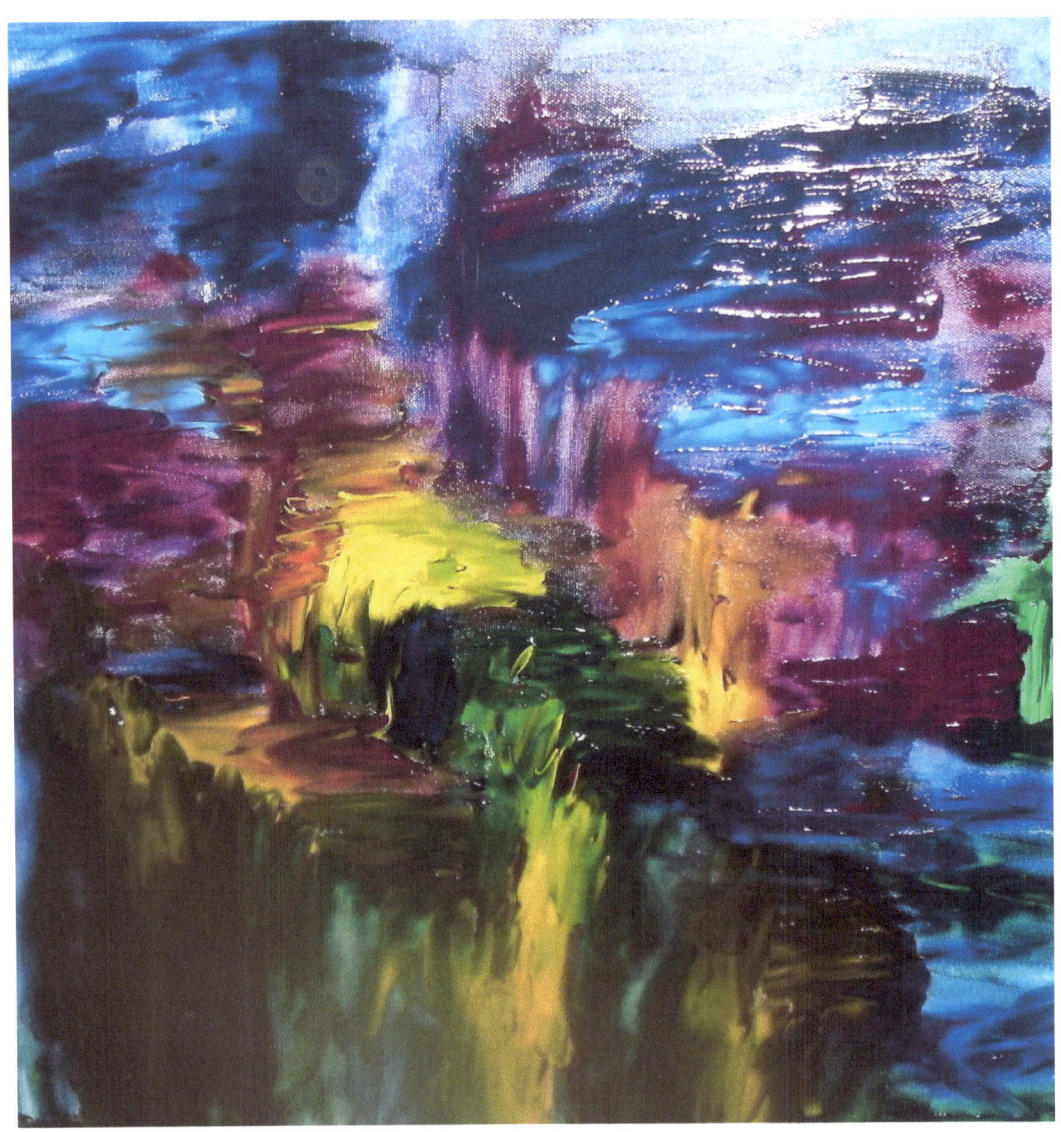

This is called infinity.This is a concept which is hard to grasp but with the best minds at work it is possible to glimpse a hopeful future in it.

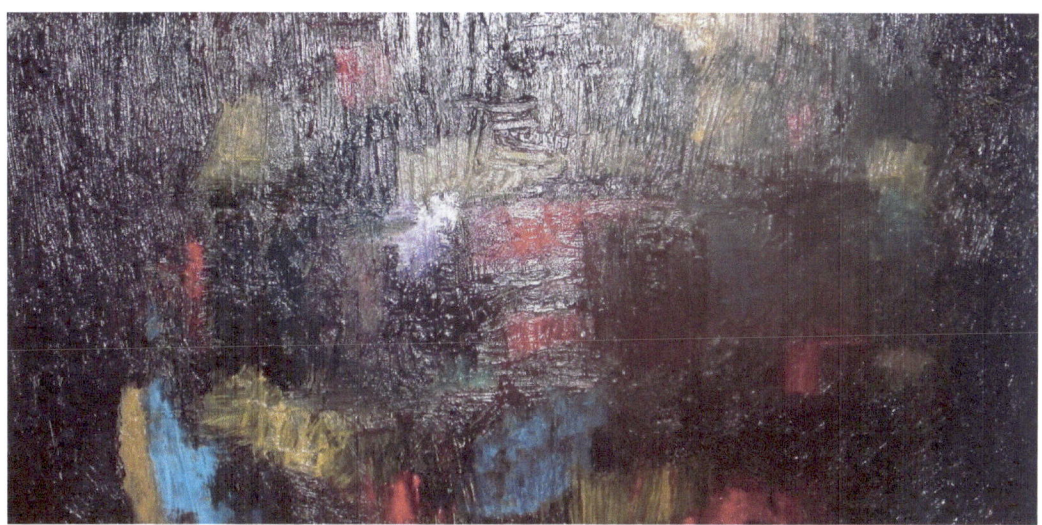

This is called prime numbers.These are very important in the structure of the mathematical universe.These can be used as signposts as certainties with which to fathom infinity.

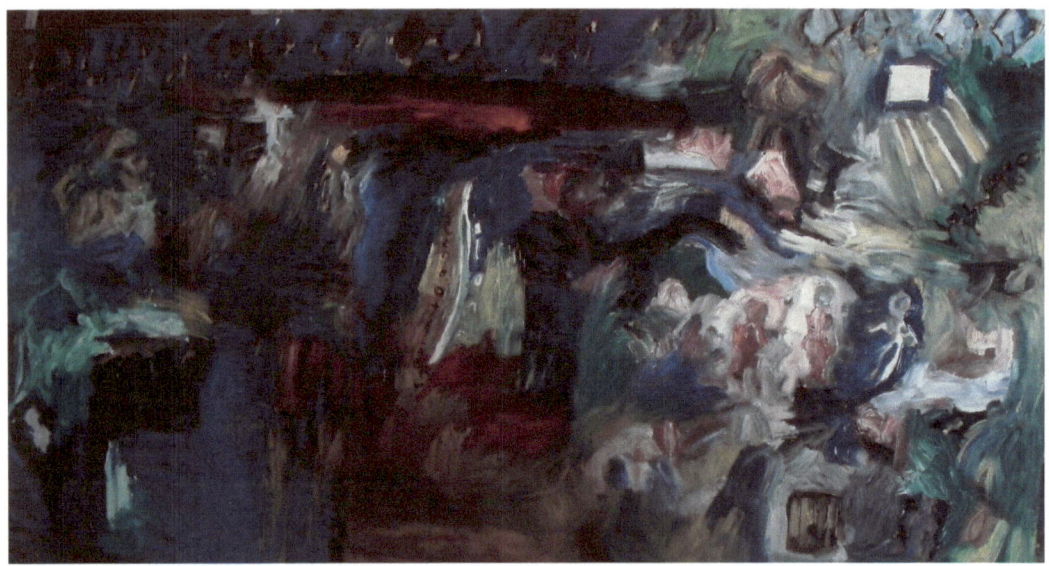

This is another possible future it is called the end of time.This is still largely what I think is unavoidable but staring this in the face every day is depressing so I'll move on to other options.

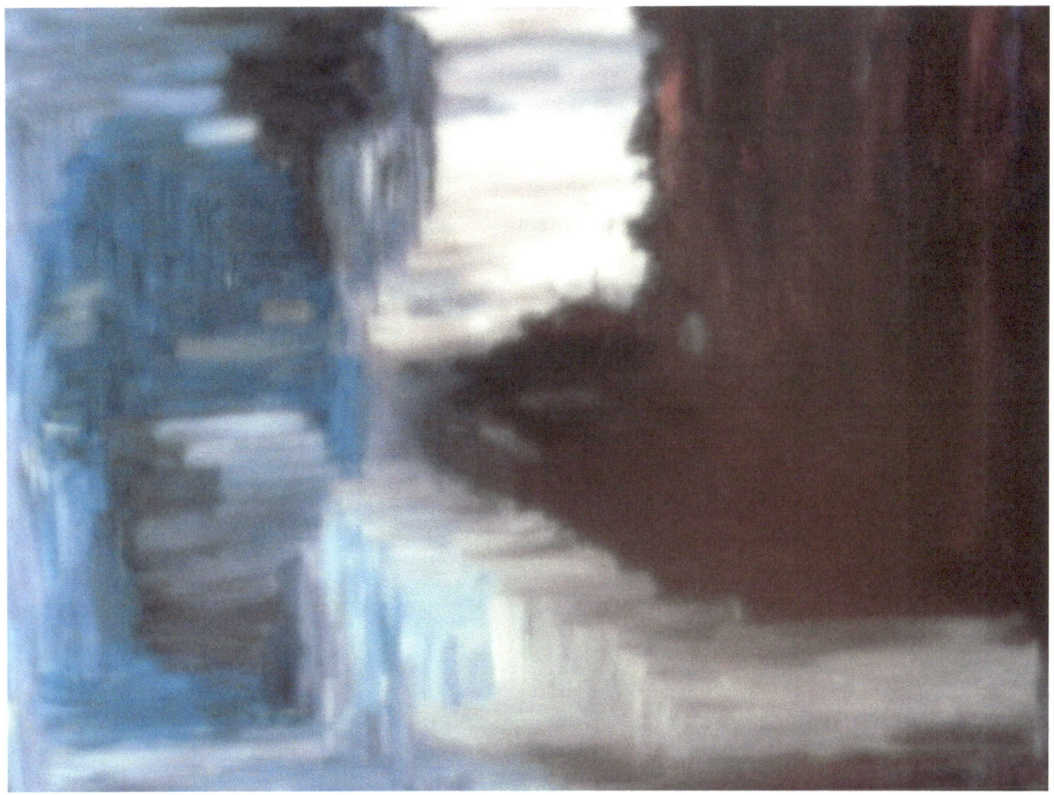

This is called metagenesis.Basically there is hope that there will be a rebirth of mankind in 2012.Some people believe that this will involve evolution into spirit bodies.Others believe they will be set free from the systems of oppression that keep them working.

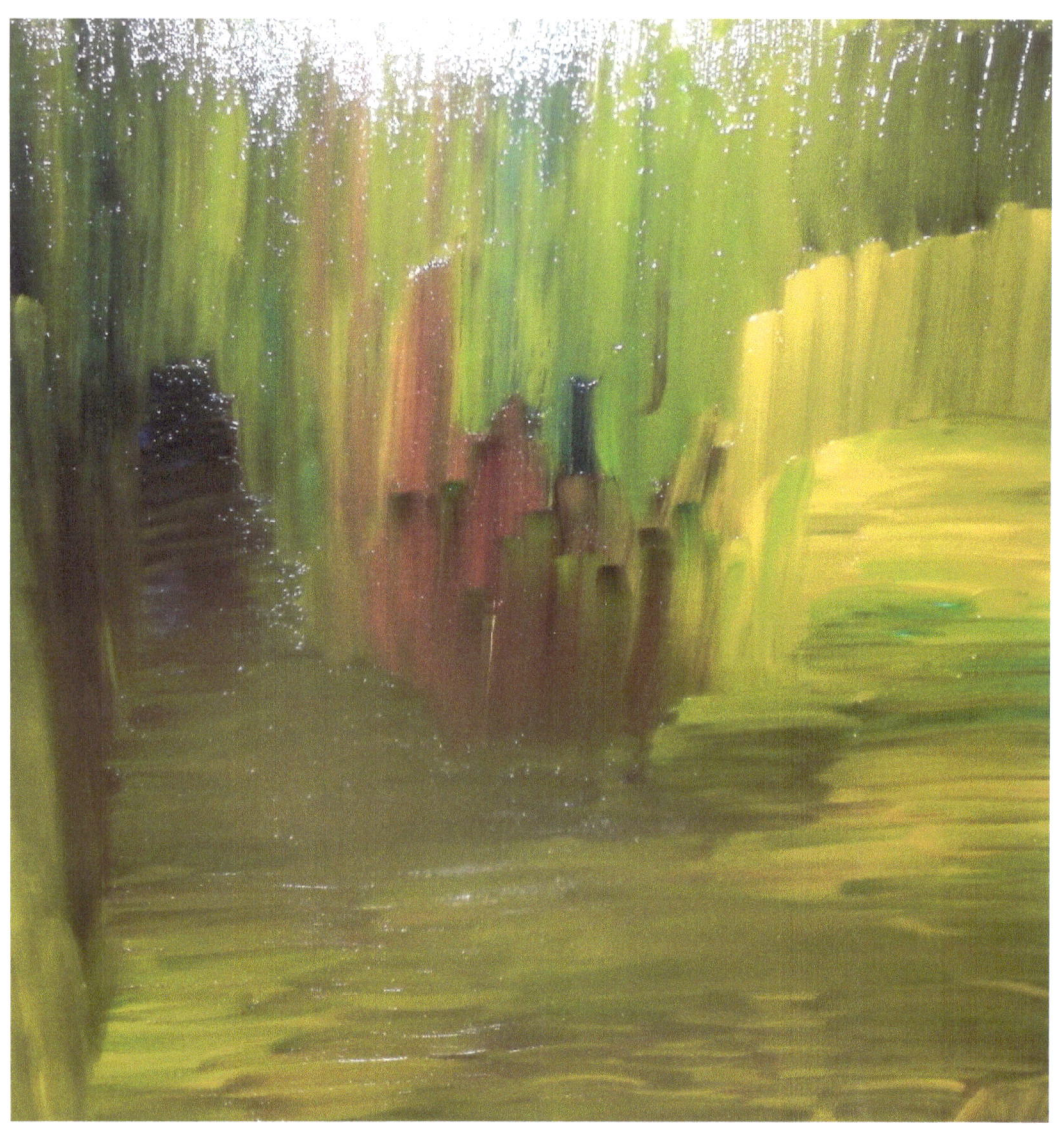

This is a vision of a far flung future called Heliopolis.It is again a possible future.

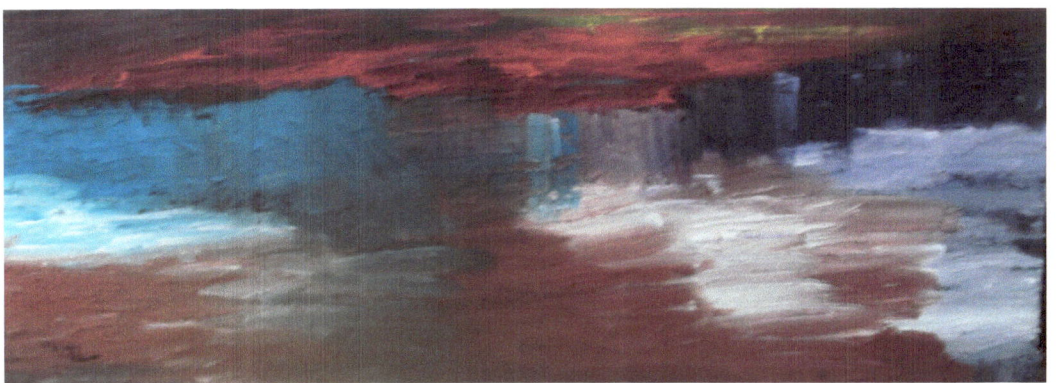

This is called the uncontrolled rain clouds appear at last and is again a glimpse of a far flung future.

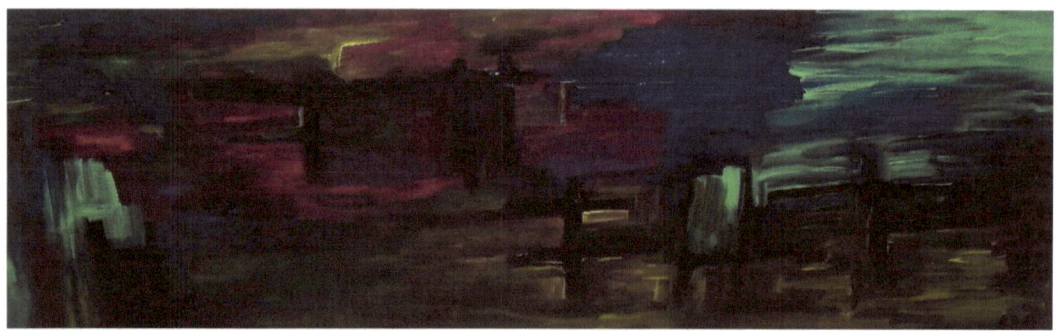

This is another possible future called future calvary.It takes place at the end of the universe and prevents its demise.As you can see there are more crosses this time.However I do not think that there is a religious solution to the problem.This ends the chapter.

Chapter three.Oblivion in
Babylon.

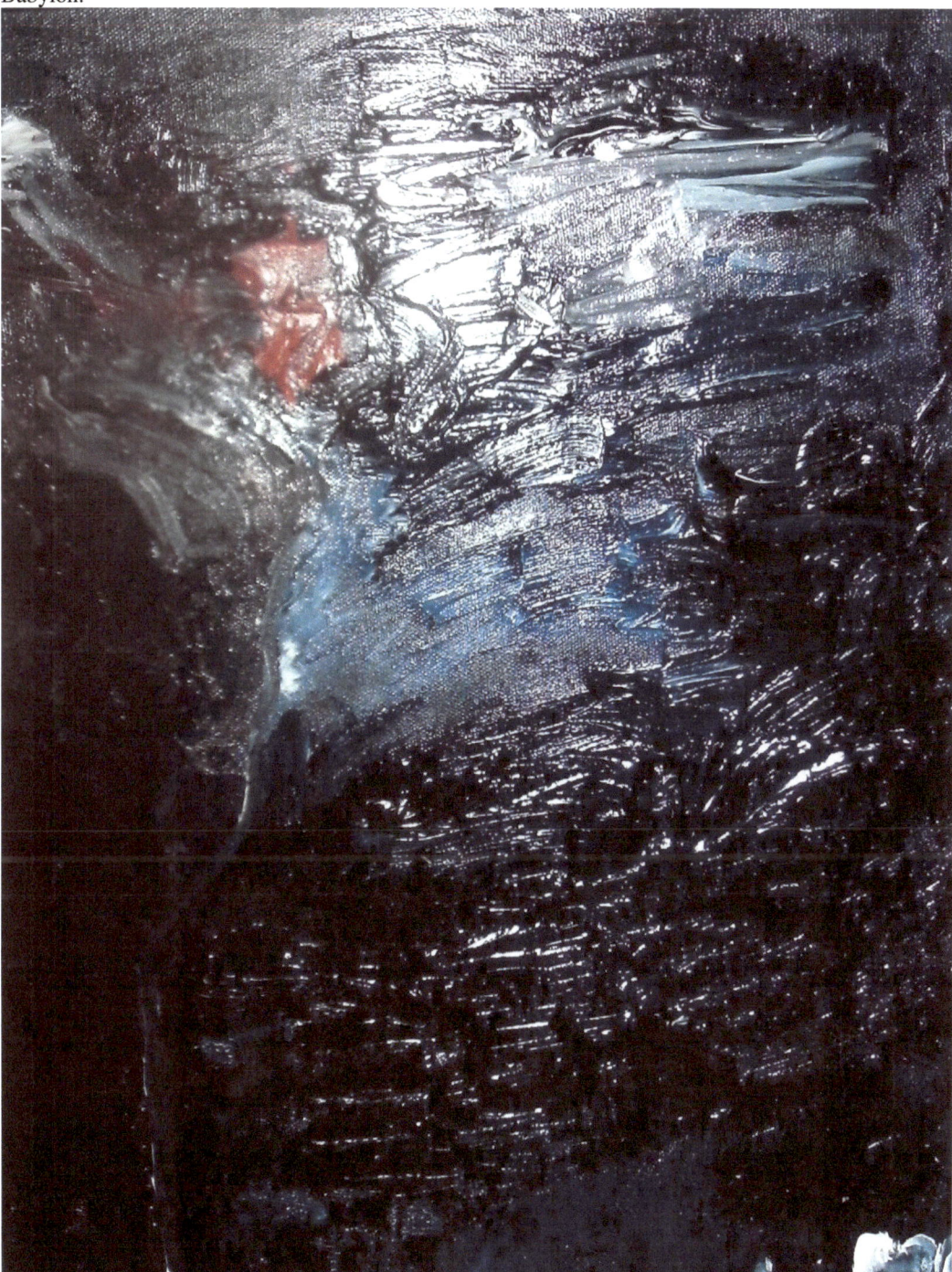

This is called John Constantine faces the dawn.

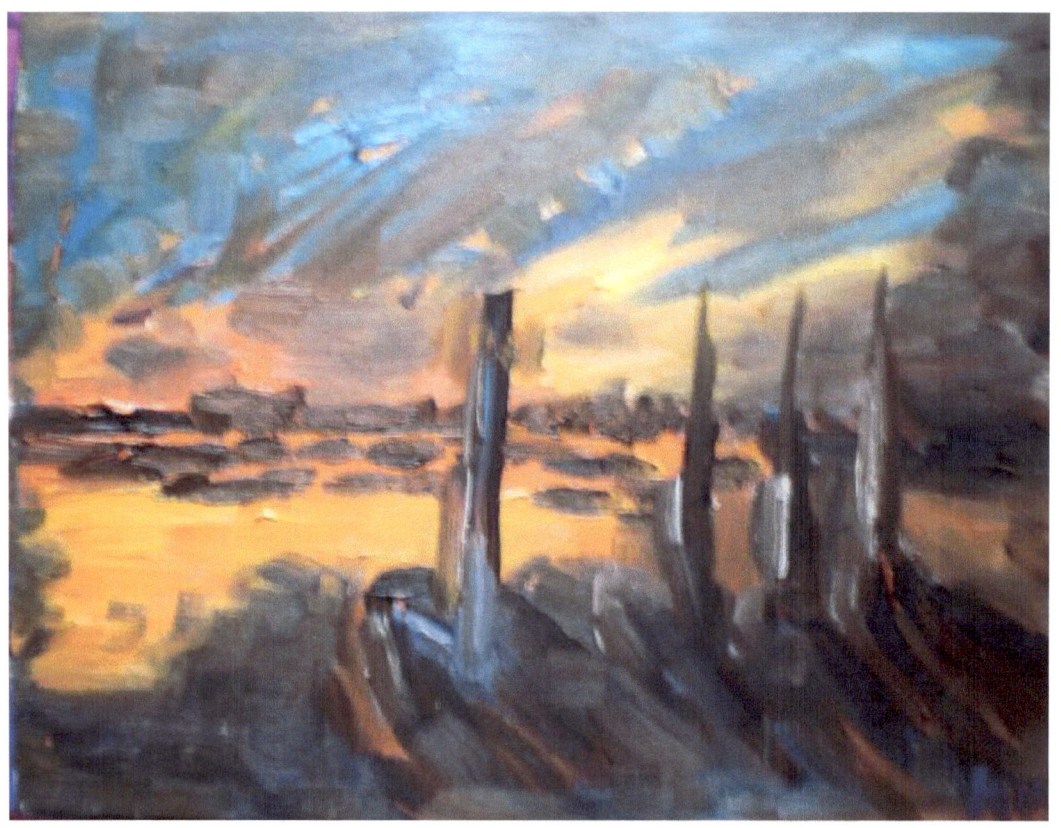

Bablon is burning with anxiety.

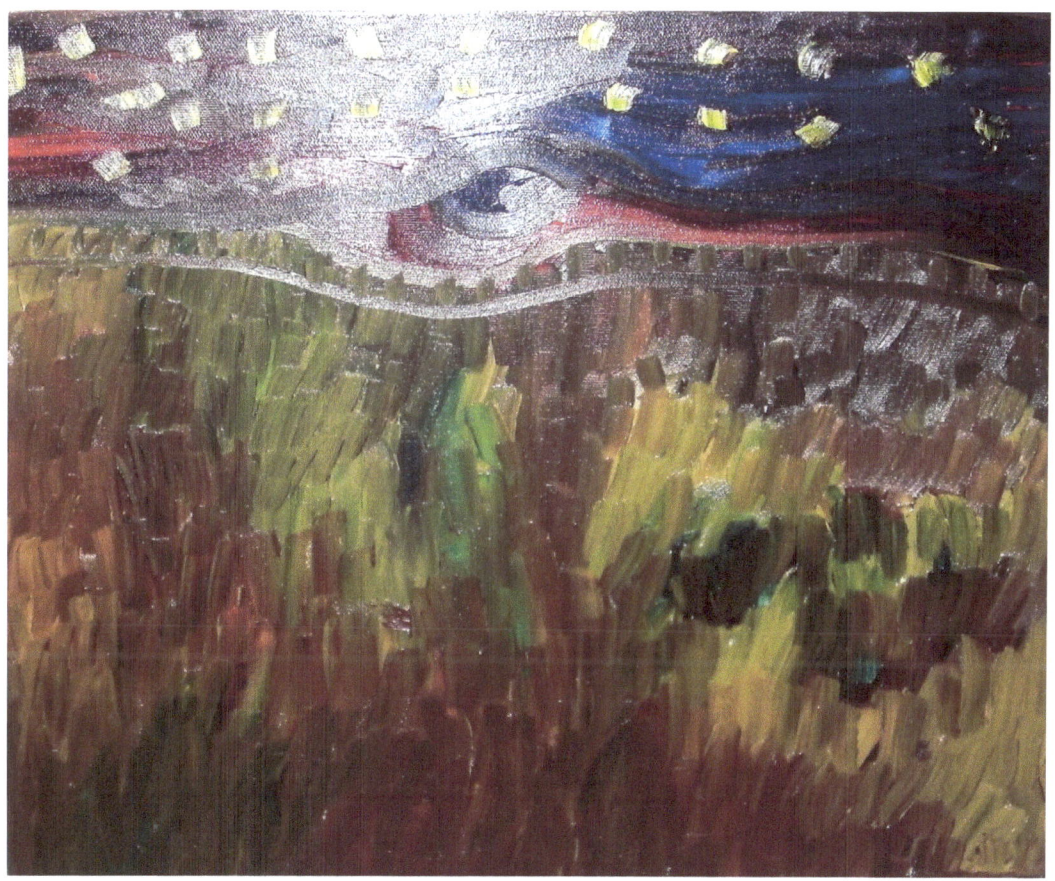

This is called field of dreams and dreams provide ways for the unconscious mind to evolve solutions.Sleeping is sometimes as important as working.Dreams drive the mindsof todays people providing respite from a cruel and heartless world.

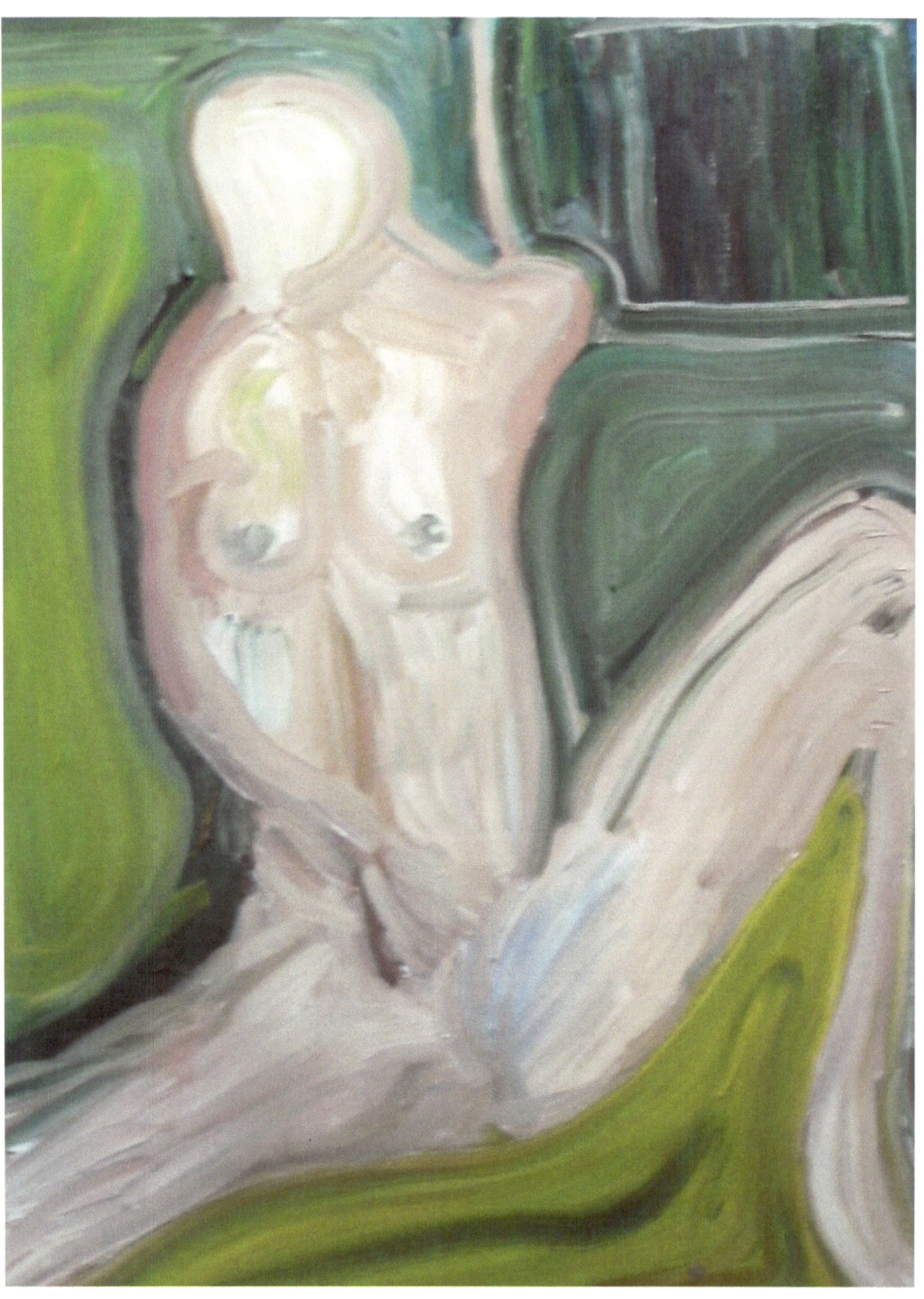

This is a pornographic painting and I believe this provided a watershed for people and a possible lowering of standards to the lowest common denominator through which people could learn how to survive in the 21st century.

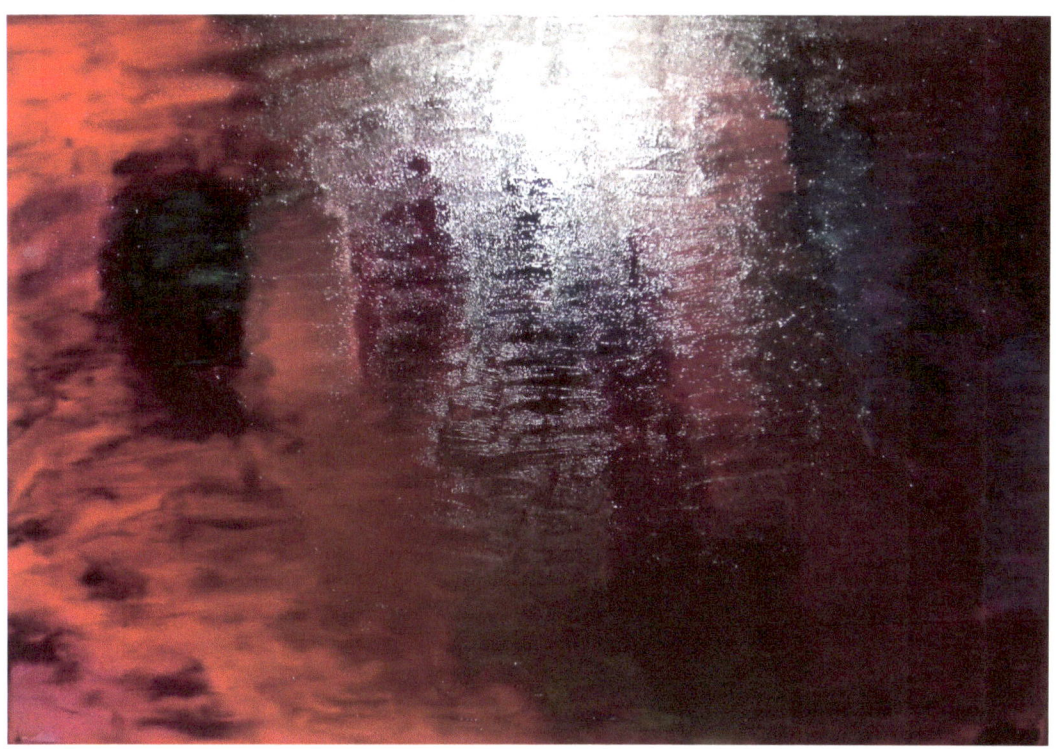

This is called city nights and cities which provide so much energy for the planet may prove to be its downfall as they suck the life out of the earth.This is the last picture of the chapter.

Chapter four.Vincent.I have come to a hypothesis that when Vincent Van Gogh shot himself the pure release of negative karma upon this world caused a door to be opened through which most of the disasters of the 20th century occurred.Here are a few of his paintings.

This is Arles from a distance.

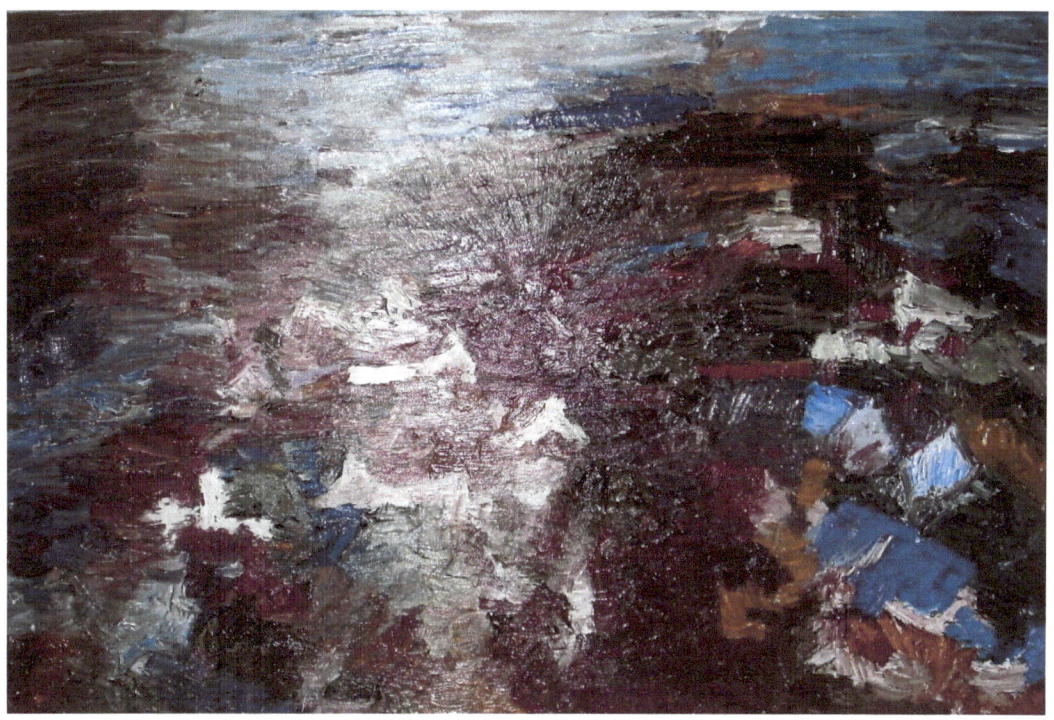

This is view of Auvers.

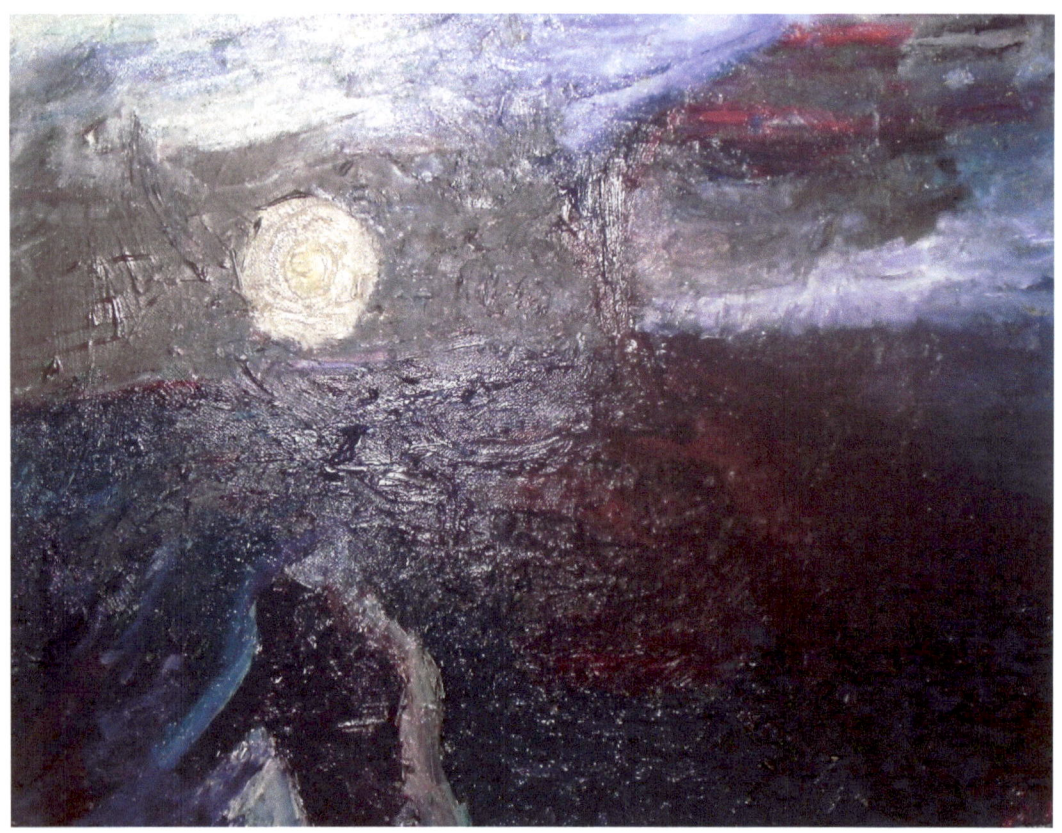

This is called The Sower

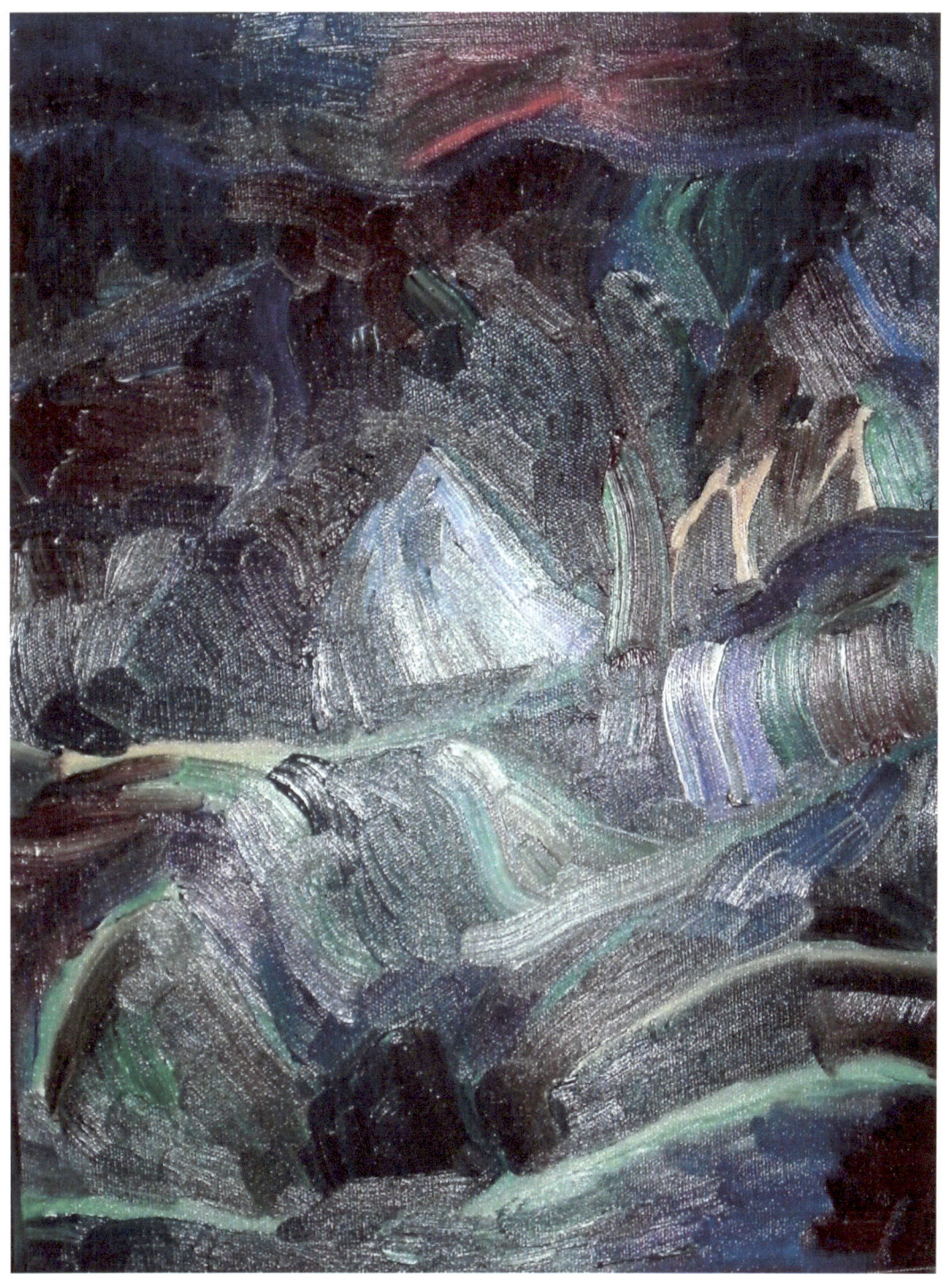

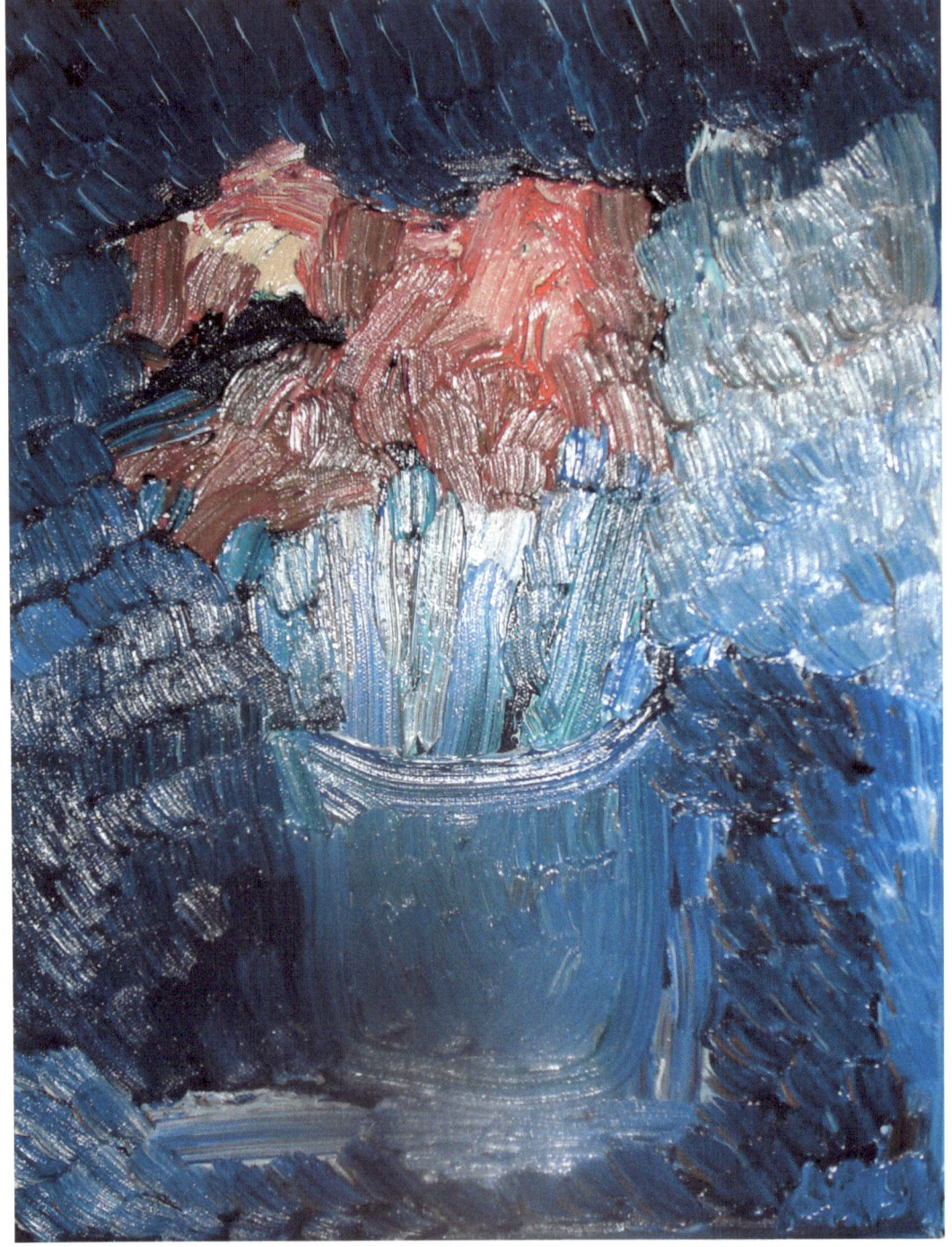

Roses

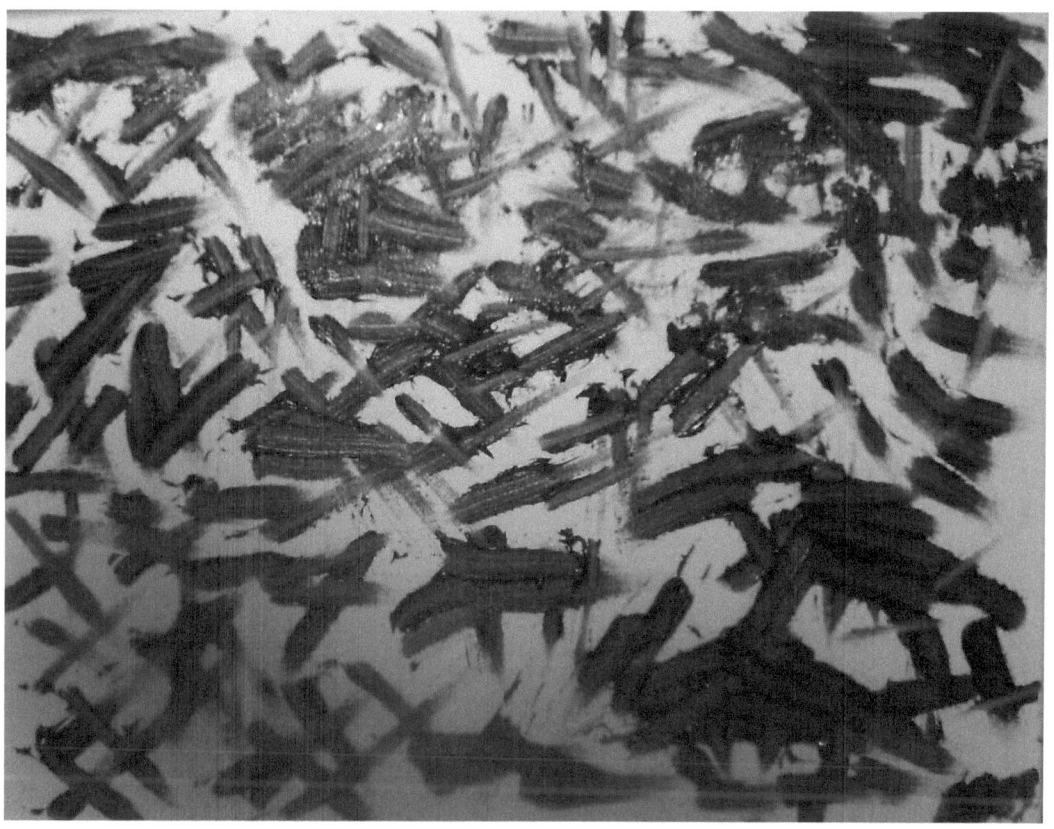

This is called blades of grass and Vincent taught us to see the future as well as beauty in simple things like this.

Chapter five.Digital heaven?Basically when digital technology was invented mankind stopped broadcasting its whereabouts in the universe to its neighbours.This was a good idea because the universe is not all light as I have previously stated.However the freedom and rawness of tv and radio became stymied so that in order to protect the earth we lost some of our freedom.

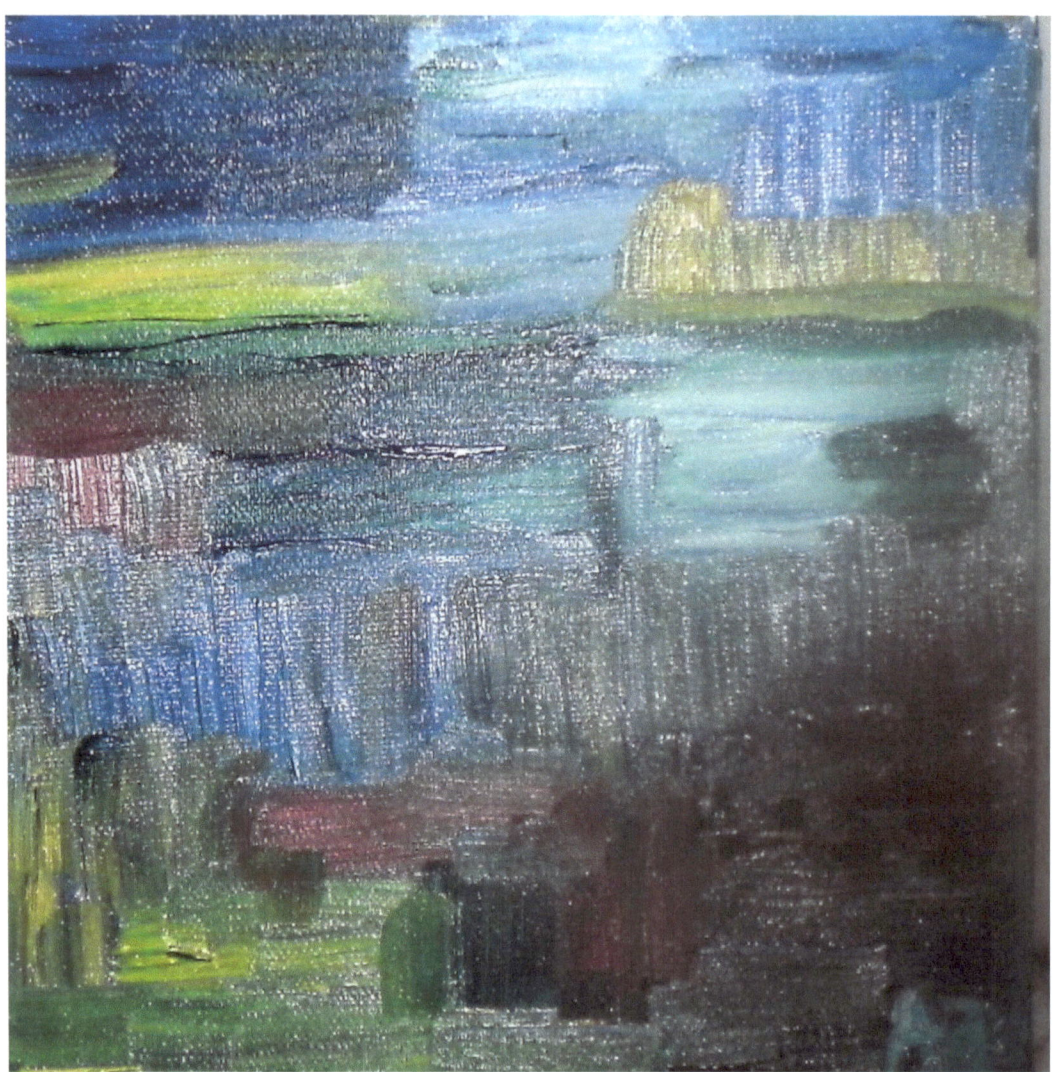

Digital Morning.

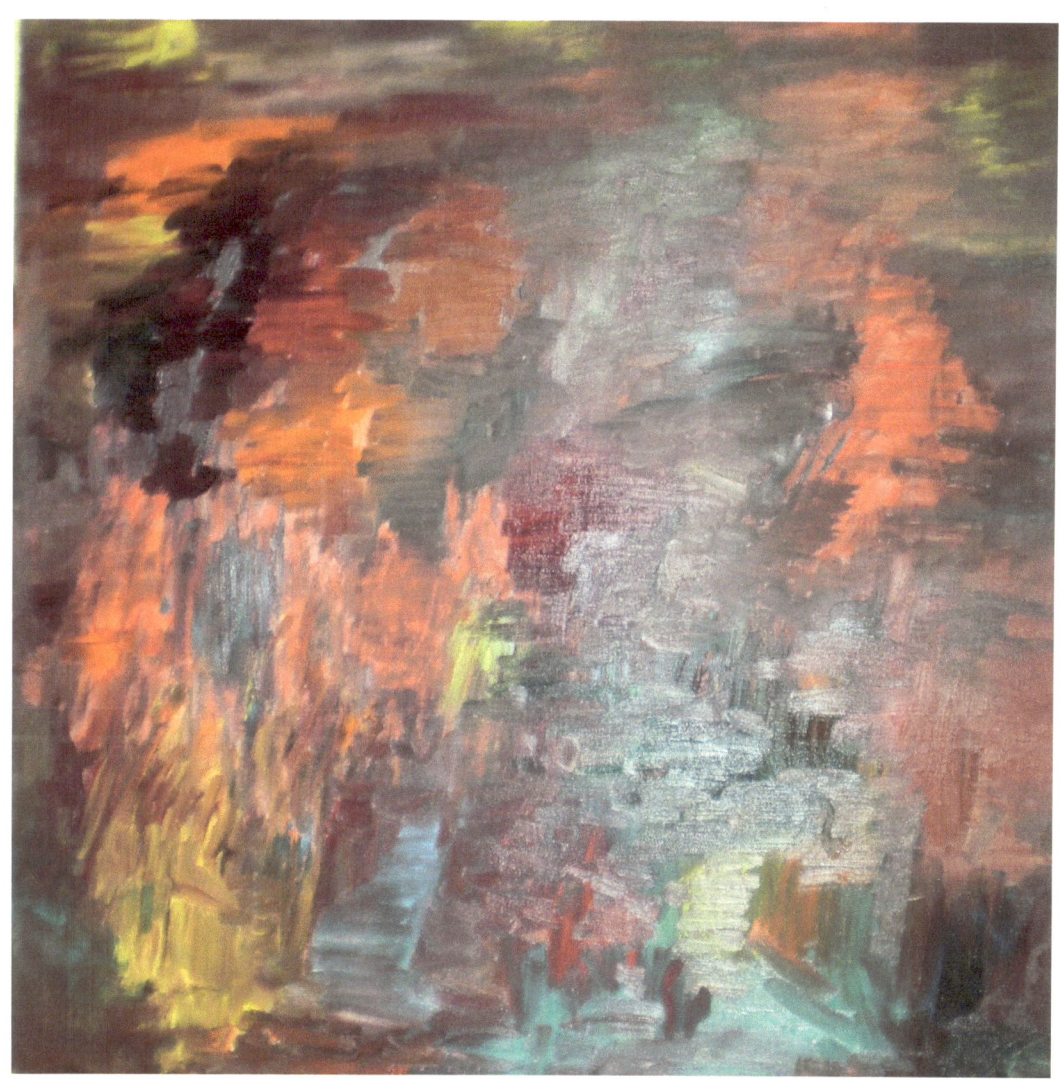

Digital Summer

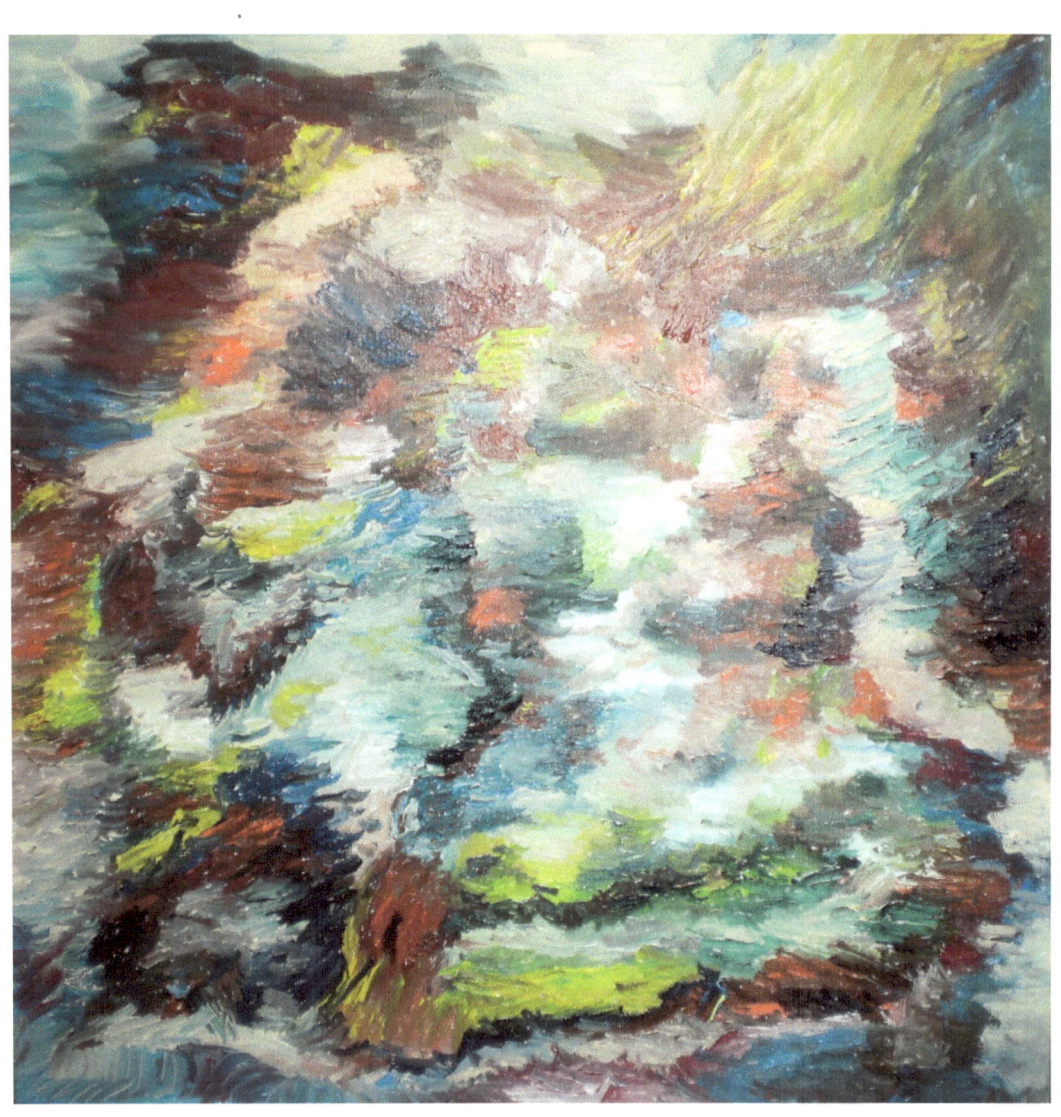

Digital China.A black hole in global terms but a good place for ideas to be born.

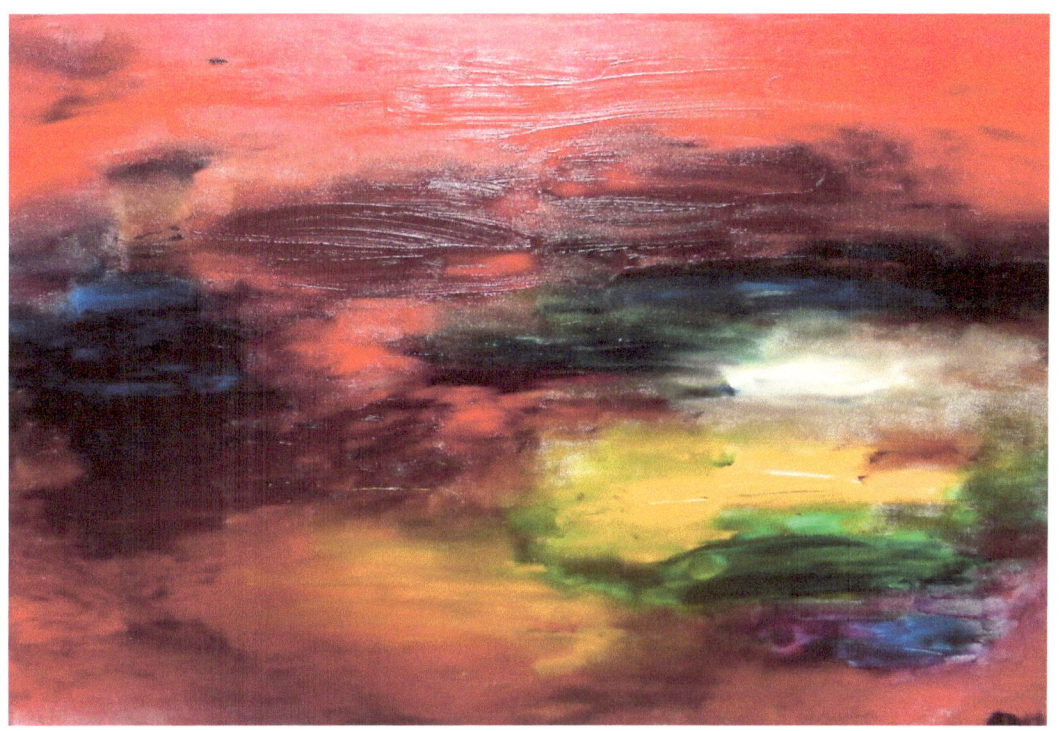

Digital Vanishing point.This is the end point.No more universe.As near to the end as I have been.It is similar in essence to future calvary.

Chapter six.Spooks.I came to their attention in about 1997.I have been trying to work as well as beat an ever hostile system which seems to want to close me down.They are basically agents for MI5 and make it hard to fulfill one's mission on earth.

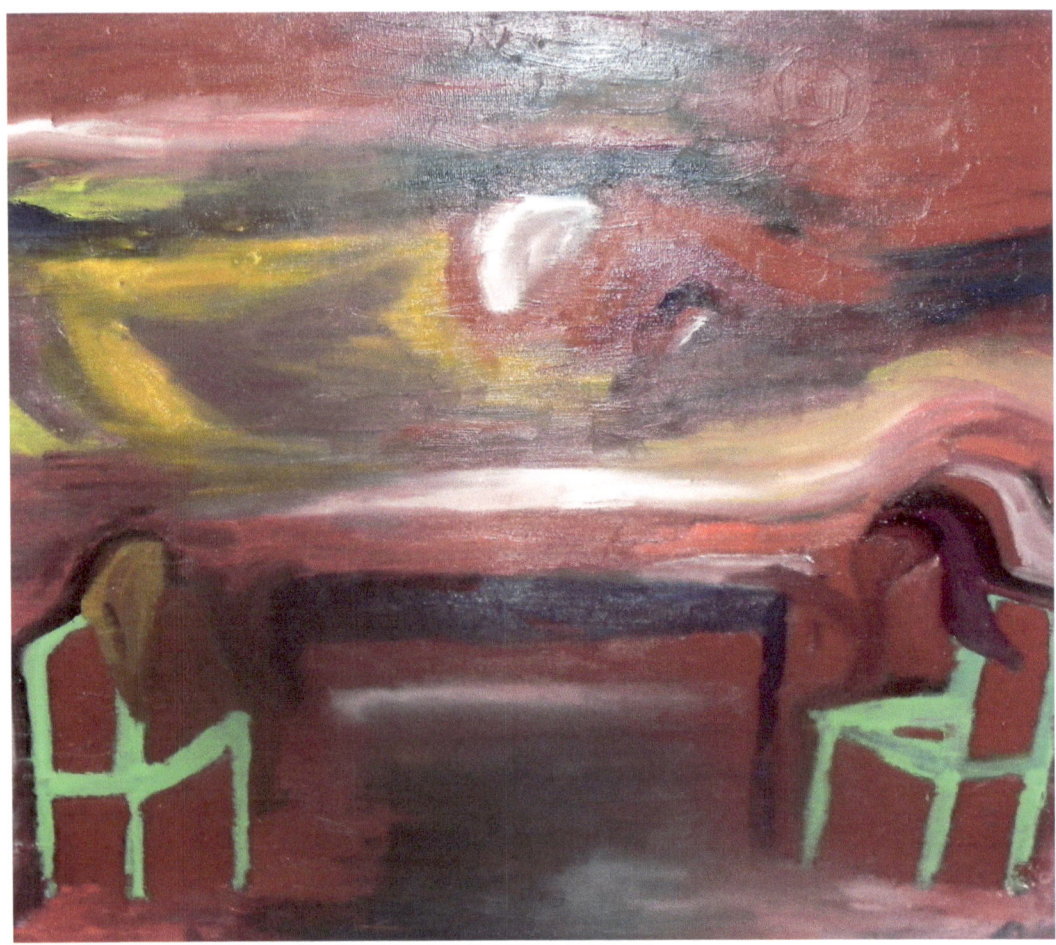

This is called shall I write to him and I heard in a letter that I was being watched.

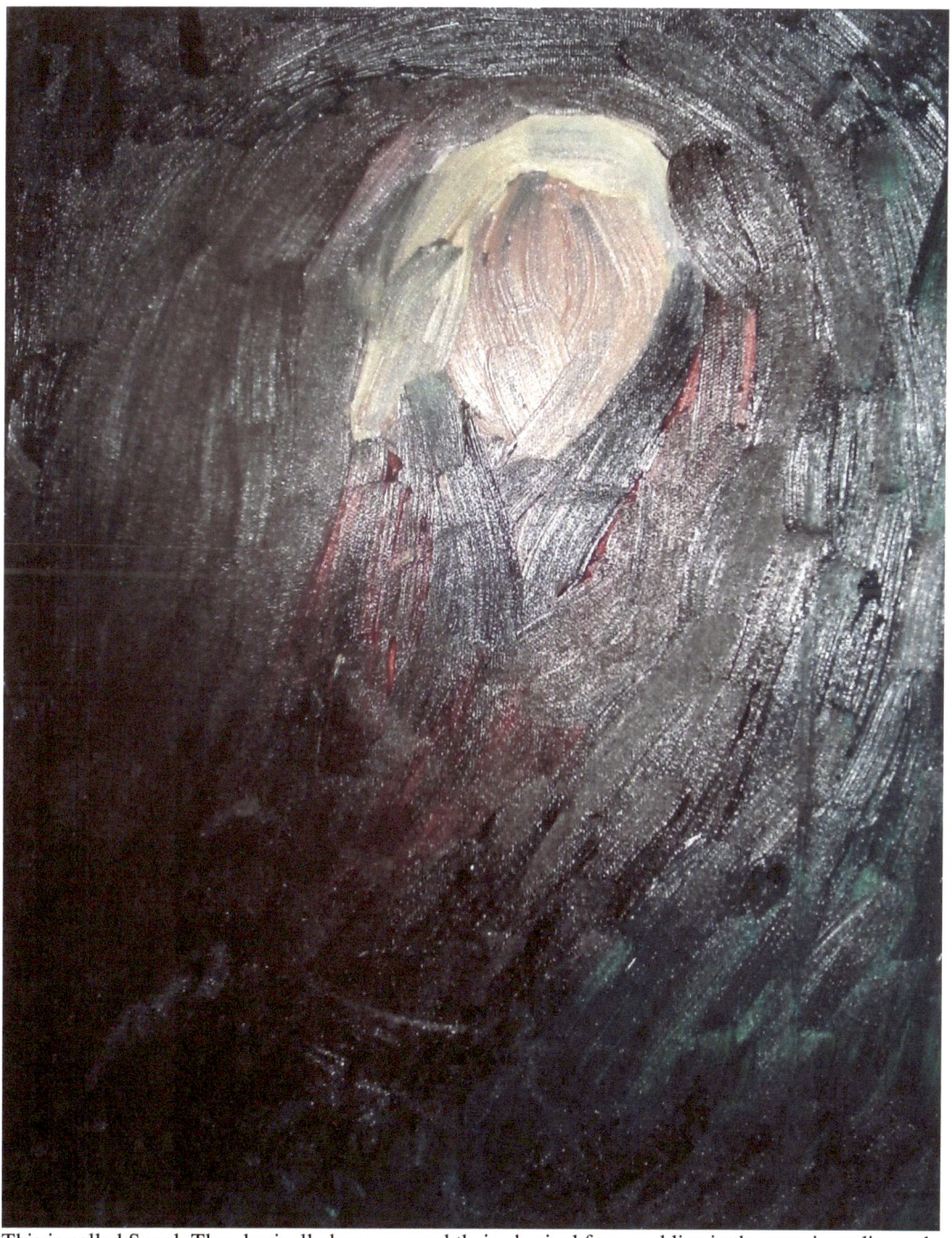

This is called Spook.They basically have escaped their physical form and live in the gaps in reality and move very quickly.

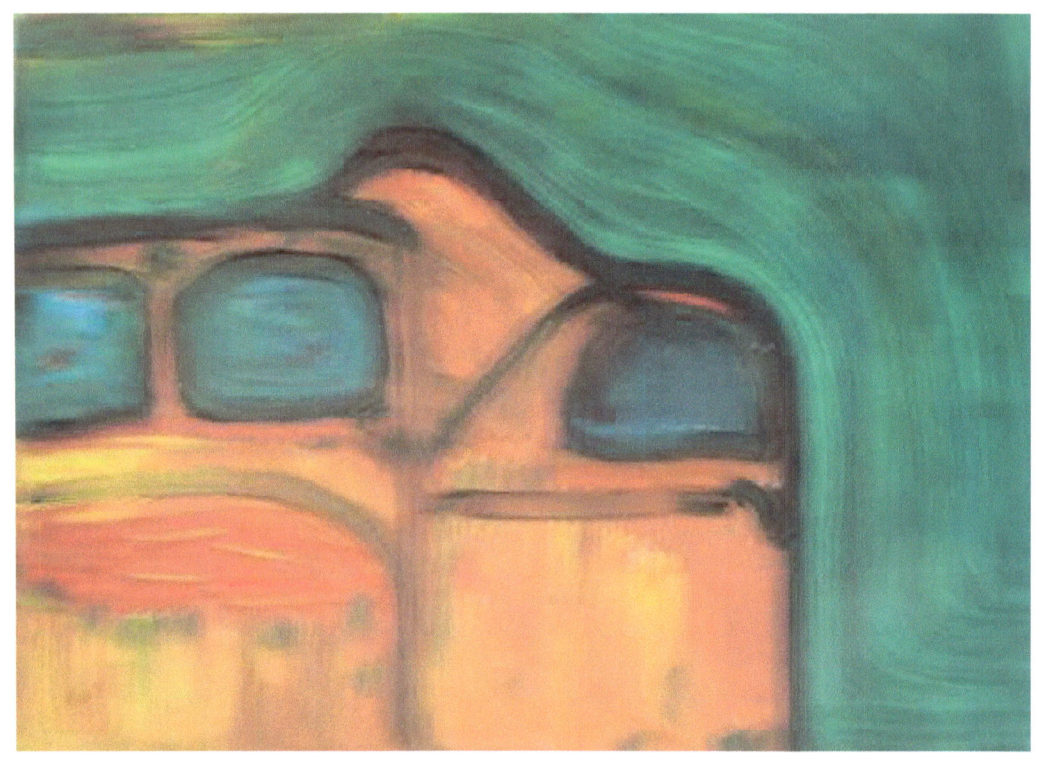

This is called Love like Death.

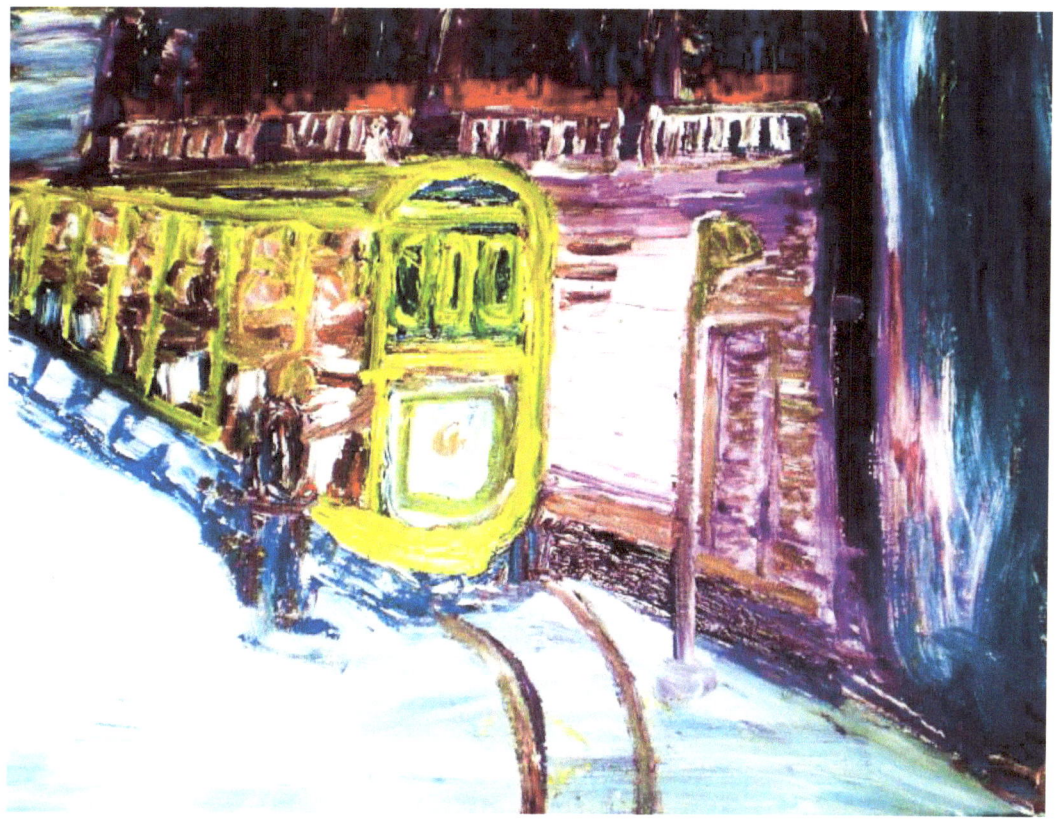

This is a picture of a tram where I first met the spook who had been tailing me.She sat opposite me and told me that she knew everything about my life.

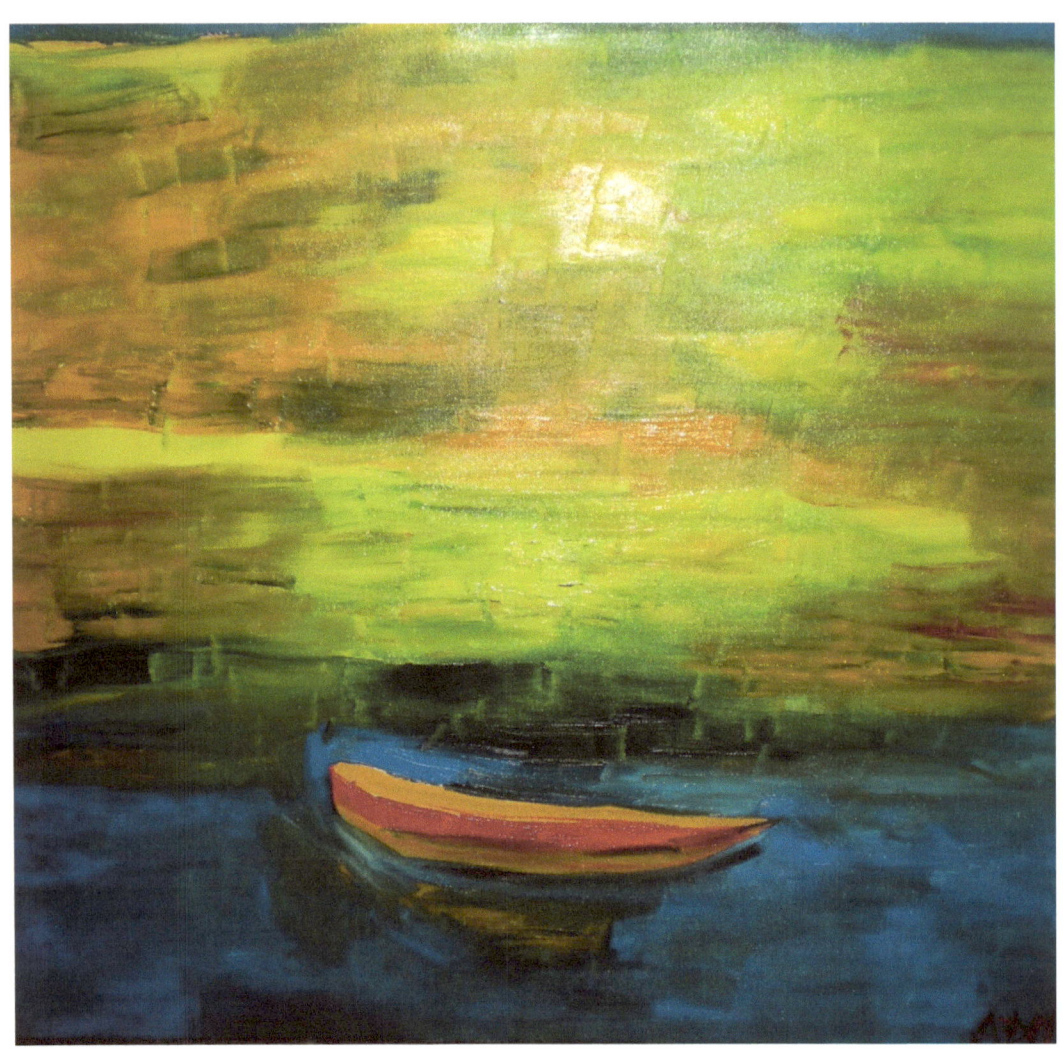

This is called beach.In the end I decided life's a beach not a bitch and gave up on an almost impossible quest to save the world when I found out that there were others far more experienced than me.Anyway, I hope that you enjoyed the book.